# INTERSPIRITUAL
# MEDITATION

## The Spiritual Paths Series

*Mandala: Creating an Authentic Spiritual Paths – An InterSpiritual Process* by Edward W. Bastian

*InterSpiritual Meditation: A Seven-Part Process from the World's Spiritual Traditions* by Edward W. Bastian

*Meditations for InterSpiritual Practice: A Collection of Practices from the World's Spiritual Traditions* by Netanel Miles-Yépez

For more information on the Spiritual Paths Institute, its programs and Spiritual Paths seminars, and as well as courses in InterSpiritual Meditation, please visit: www.spiritualpaths.net / www.interspiritualmeditation.org.

# INTERSPIRITUAL MEDITATION

*A Seven-Step Process Drawn from the World's Spiritual Traditions*

Second Edition

## EDWARD W. BASTIAN

Edited by
Netanel Miles-Yépez

*The Spiritual Paths Series*

Albion
*Andalus*

Boulder, Colorado
*2015*

*"The old shall be renewed,*
*and the new shall be made holy."*
— Rabbi Avraham Yitzhak Kook

Albion-Andalus Inc.
P. O. Box 19852
Boulder, CO 80308
*www.albionandalus.com*

Design and composition by Albion-Andalus Inc.
Cover design by Sari Wisenthal-Shore.
The "Flower of InterSpiritual Meditation" on the cover envisioned
by Edward W. Bastian and created by Lynda Rae.
Photos of Edward W. Bastian by Charles Abbott and Michael
Stinson.

Manufactured in the United States of America

ISBN-13: 978-0692378434 (Albion-Andalus Books)
ISBN-10: 069237843X

*I dedicate this book*
*To Gardeners of Consciousness,*
*Who nurture the seeds of*
*Wisdom and compassion*
*So that others' minds*
*Might ripen to their full potential.*

*To courageous contemplatives,*
*Meditators in all traditions,*
*Who patiently persevere*
*Amidst all difficulties*
*To experience their truths*
*Then open to the wisdom of others*
*To discover a common ground*
*For universal peace and enlightenment.*

*To those who have experienced*
*The bliss of enlightenment*
*Then re-engage in the world*
*To help others find their own paths*
*To freedom and service.*

*May the seed of enlightenment*
*Ripen in all beings.*

To His Holiness the Dalai Lama, Father Thomas Keating, and Rabbi Zalman Schachter-Shalomi, master teachers of meditation and openers of the way to InterSpirituality. To Geshe Lhundup Sopa, who guided me along the Buddhist path, and advised me with these words: "Do not teach what you do not know."

# CONTENTS

"*Humanity stands at a crossroads between horror and hope. In choosing hope, we must seed a new consciousness, a radically fresh approach to life drawing its inspiration from perennial spiritual and moral insights, intuition and experience. We call this new awareness* interspiritual, *implying not the homogenization of religion, but the recovering of the shared mystic heart beating in the center of the world's deepest spiritual traditions.*"

— Attributed to Brother Wayne Teasdale

# PREFACE

IN 1970, AFTER YEARS of hitchhiking around the world and exploring different careers, I decided to change the course of my life and pursue a spiritual journey. By conventional standards, I was well on my way to becoming 'a success.' After all, I had been a college basketball player, worked as a writer for NBC, a photojournalist in Vietnam, a documentary filmmaker in Africa, and political organizer for congressional and presidential campaigns.

By my own measures of success, I was on my way to a happy and fulfilling life. But when I really took an honest look at the unhappy lives of my bosses and role models at the time, I just didn't want to end up like them. While they had the accoutrements of success and power, they didn't have the wisdom and compassion to improve the state of the world or the inner quality of their own lives.

I had seen enough to know that 'sex, drugs and rock 'n' roll,' or the more adult preoccupations with fame, money, and possessions, weren't going to satisfy my longing for something deeper and more satisfying. So I moved from the hustle 'n' bustle of New York City to the open grandeur of the Rocky Mountains near Aspen, Colorado and adopted an entirely different lifestyle. At the time, I wasn't necessarily looking for anything 'spiritual,' I was just trying to find greater meaning and purpose in my life. I became a part-time landscaper, schoolteacher and started a video ski instruction service. I also began reading and exploring the great works of philosophy and spirituality. I spent my summers living in a tent near mountain streams and integrating my psyche into the elements and forces of nature. For the first time, I felt that I was setting my own course in life and truly appreciated for the person I aspired to become.

Nevertheless, I also found that even the exhilaration of mountain living wasn't sufficient. I had successfully transplanted myself in a new life, yet my persistent quest for life-meaning and purpose had come along for the ride. That's when it finally dawned on me—happiness couldn't possibly come from outside myself, no matter how much I changed my outward circumstances. I would have to make an internal change as well.

As if by magic, the perfect opportunity arose in response to my new realization. I was invited to work with the famous journalist and broadcaster, Lowell Thomas. I was to accompany him to Nepal and then to Dharamsala, India, to interview and film His Holiness, the 14th Dalai Lama, the temporal and spiritual leader of Tibet in exile. I had already begun reading about Buddhism, and now I hoped to ask my own questions of a true spiritual leader.

During these interviews, I was immediately struck by the Dalai Lama's warmth and personable manner, and still more by the fact that—though he was only nine years my senior—he radiated a kind of peace I had never seen before. He even seemed interested in me, and I was privileged to have a number of private interviews with him just as I had hoped. He asked about the issues that were important to me, and we talked about American youth and their desire for political change, about the war in Vietnam and what I had seen there. When we had covered all these topics, I summoned the courage to tell him about my own disillusionment with religion and my personal struggles to find a purpose and some wisdom and peace of mind. It was then that he began to give me my first formal teachings on the central concepts of Buddhism.

His teachings and our in-depth conversations gave me the courage to look at the human condition head-on—with all of its beauty and ugliness—and to see that my present approach to happiness was only creating more suffering in my life. But, at first, I was puzzled by the apparent paradox of what he was saying. This must have showed on my face, because he then began to demonstrate, clearly and concisely, how genuine happiness must come from *meditation, wisdom,* and *compassion.* Then he provided me with introductions to the teachers who would then guide my studies and practice.

The first of these was Geshe Rabten, whom he called his "Junior Tutor." It was he who first introduced me to Buddhist meditation. His Holiness also advised me to continue my studies with Geshe Lhundup Sopa, one of the finest scholars of his generation, who would become my academic and spiritual teacher. It was he who personally guided my Buddhist practice for the next fourteen years, as well as my doctoral work in Buddhist Studies at the University of Wisconsin.

Since that time, meditation has become one of the cornerstones of my life. My experiences with it (and with Buddhist practice generally) have convinced me that each of us has within us a potential for unlimited wisdom, compassion, and happiness. It is meditation that makes the difference—a meditation done in the context of a spiritual path and alignment with our individual spiritual styles and questions.

Buddhism teaches that our consciousness, with all its pure and impure qualities, incarnates in new bodies, life-after-life, seeking liberation and enlightenment, attempting to uncover the pure Buddha Nature inherent in us. But one doesn't need to be a Buddhist, or to believe in reincarnation, to take advantage of meditation. It seems that all the world's great spiritual traditions have similar notions about this sacred potential of our innermost being. Only, instead of Buddha Nature, it might be called the Holy Spirit, the Divine Indwelling, Divine Love, or Christ Consciousness. Likewise, many of these traditions, in one way or another, teach us that this sacred potential can expand to pervade our entire being, if we will only engage wholeheartedly in spiritual practice.

For myself, I can say with some assurance that I have gradually found much of what I was seeking when I first brought my questions to the Dalai Lama all those years ago. It is not 'happiness' as I would have defined it before I came to Dharamsala, but something more profound and satisfying. Dedicated spiritual practice has slowly awakened in me the possibility of a genuine compassion for all beings, and a sustainable peace of mind. It has changed the way in which I view reality. It has helped to ground me in life's profound purposes and given a new depth to my personal relationships.

This is not a boast, as my own journey is still far from complete. It is simply my own report about a life that has changed for the better. Nor do I mean to overstate my own meditative abilities and experiences. I am quite certain they are, at best, modest in comparison with my teachers and role models. Even after forty-five years, I still feel I am only a beginner. My own delicate meditative tranquility and slowly evolving insights are continual reminders of this fact. But perhaps this is the 'proof' of meditation's effectiveness. For in spite of my own shortcomings, my internal life has nevertheless been transformed into something richer and more vibrant than it would have been had I not begun this journey.

After years of intense study and practice of Buddhism, I began working with some of the finest meditation teachers from the world's great spiritual traditions. This book is a product of both my own personal training in Buddhism and my experience of studying, meditating, and teaching with these wonderful representatives of their traditions. Meditation itself requires constant effort. It is not easy to sit still, to sit regularly, or to sustain inner silence amidst the cacophony of daily life. But the purpose of this book is not to suggest that it is 'easy,' or that there are just 'seven simple steps to enlightenment,' but to provide you with seven insights and possibilities for making your meditation more personally *effective,* as well as *affective.* It is a non-sectarian contemplative process that people of different religions and spiritual traditions—as well as people without a tradition—can do together to improve the quality of their lives, and to find new solutions to the challenges of our times.

Since the first edition of this book was published in 2010, I have used it widely in my classes and retreats. Thus, this new edition contains some of what I have learned since then. It is also augmented by two companion books: *Meditations for InterSpiritual Practice* and *Mandala: Creating an Authentic Spiritual Path: An InterSpiritual Process.* The first provides helpful articles and guided meditations from distinguished spiritual teachers of many different traditions. While the second provides a systematic process for discerning and harnessing your spiritual styles and questions in the creation of your own personal path and contemplative practice.

While I have been deeply blessed by the friendship and advice of many excellent teachers, they are of course not responsible for my errors or omissions. I am just one of many trying to find our collective way into the meaning and promise of the InterSpiritual legacy left to us by great teachers and elders throughout the ages. May this work be an oar-stroke toward the fulfillment of this prophetic and collaborative vision.

DR. EDWARD W. BASTIAN
*Aboard "Uma Karuna,"*
*Santa Barbara Harbor, California, 2014*

# INTRODUCTION

*IN THE TIME OF KING SHUDDHODANA, it was foretold that his son, Prince Siddhartha, would become a great king, indeed the ruler of a vast empire—but only if he could be prevented from seeing old age, sickness, and death. Now, because the king wished his son to follow in his footsteps, and to become an even greater ruler than himself, he used all his power to protect his son from the vicissitudes of life. Both day and night, prince Siddhartha was surrounded by young and healthy people and many beautiful things. There was nothing near him that he might dash his foot against. But the prince quickly grew bored with everything he saw, and looked ever to see what was outside of the palace gates. Finally, he called a charioteer to take him on a tour of the city. His father tried to prevent this in various ways, creating fictional scenes upon the streets and trying to entice his son with still greater pleasures, but nothing worked. For on each outing, prince Siddhartha was shocked by a sight he had never seen before: an old man in an alley, a sick woman being cared for by others, and finally, a dead body being carried to its funeral. Then he saw the strangest site of all, a shaven headed man in the robes of a monk meditating in the park. So compelling was this man's silent absorption and true majesty that the prince decided then and there to seek a new life, a new path to happiness.*

WE ALL YEARN FOR HAPPINESS, for peace of mind, to find the answers to life's most basic questions—*Who am I? What will become of me?* These questions are woven into the fabric of our very nature, as if we were genetically programmed to seek the answers to them. At the same time, we also need to survive: to feed and clothe ourselves, to find shelter for our bodies and our families, to form communities of mutual support. To live, we must enmesh ourselves in the interdependent matrix of all life, while at the same time, adapting ourselves to the frequently opposing pulls of both meaning and survival. For serving both of these ends turns out to be critical, not only for our own health, but also for the health of those who depend on us.

But for all our yearning and seeking, we have to admit, most of us are not as happy as we would like to be. We have so little peace of mind in the face of life's necessities, and the answers to life's big questions continue to elude us in a game of hide-and-seek. Like young prince Siddhartha (who would later become the Buddha), we are often shocked by our own powerlessness before illnesses, aging, and death. Moreover, we find that in order to feed and clothe ourselves, we must harm or kill other beings; to warm and cool our homes, we must deplete our natural resources and poison the environment; to transport our bodies from one place to another, we must pollute the air. How could we be happy in the face of such dilemmas?

For many people, the search for happiness and peace of mind requires an ever-increasing abundance of comforts and sensual pleasures. We build more and more walls to insulate ourselves (and those we love) from the basic facts of our existence. As we strive to get more money, to buy better insurance, to build bigger houses, eating more food than we need, filling our days with entertainment and endless stimulation, we are still unable to buffer our minds against our ever-changing reality. Just as with prince Siddhartha, our desire to protect ourselves merely sets-up a greater shock and disappointment when *life* actually happens and we experience impermanence in the midst of all our delusions of safety. Strangely enough, it is this shocking confrontation with reality that finally forces us to look in a new direction.

MEDITATION

Now, if these external things cannot bring us the peace and happiness we desire—a fact for which we have daily testimony—then peace and happiness must come from within. But how do we begin to get at them? How do we begin to open this inner treasury?

One answer, suggested by many spiritual teachers over millennia, is meditation done in the context of a genuine spiritual path. Meditation, it is said, helps us to rest calmly in the essence of our being, allowing us to move through the world with an inner stillness, contentment, and a compassionate empathy. In the depths of meditative awareness, we find ourselves connected to the essential nature of all beings. We realize that our own welfare is intimately connected with that of others; so we are compelled to help them as we would help ourselves. Thus, meditation (along with other complimentary practices) is a key for unlocking the inner treasury of personal peace and happiness.

But what is meditation? There is so much talk of it today, and yet so little awareness of its actual processes and intended effects. Adding to the confusion is the fact that there are so many different methods of meditation: some which focus on the breath, others which involve visualizations or contemplation of sacred concepts, and many which are solely occupied with the chanting of words, phrases, or sacred syllables. Moreover, it is not always clear whether the word 'meditation' refers to a technique or the result of that technique. Some have even begun to wonder whether that technique is spiritual or scientific, or whether the result is sacred or biochemical. Some of these questions you will obviously have to answer for yourself, but many, I hope, will become clear in the course of your reading this book.

Suffice it to say for now: Meditation is a technique for attuning consciousness, which—depending on the individual, the technique used, and the spiritual context in which it is done—may lead to altered states of awareness (including, profound focus and tranquility), usually considered beneficial or transformative for individuals and groups.

In this book, we are working on the assumption that meditation is in fact beneficial and may lead to a positive transformation in our lives. The question of whether one technique is better than another, or if different techniques lead to different ends, is of much less importance; for I am more concerned with making the practice of meditation more personally affective, and with offering a new possibility for group meditation between seekers of different spiritual traditions, and even for those without a spiritual tradition.

## INTERSPIRITUALITY

At the core of this book is the idea of InterSpirituality, what is often described as "the shared mystic heart beating in the center of the world's deepest spiritual traditions." This term, which was introduced by Brother Wayne Teasdale in his book *The Mystic*

*Heart,* captures the essence of the next phase of global spiritual interaction. It is also critical for understanding the purpose of this book. It is not, for instance, a book on Buddhist as opposed to Christian meditation, but rather a book on the InterSpiritual process of meditation. What does this mean? It means that I, like many others, have found that there are similar structures, techniques, and common assumptions upon which the world's spiritual traditions have based and evolved their own meditative practices; that the particular practices of these traditions have evolved individually as well as in relationship to each other as they have come into contact over the millennia.

There are a marvelously profound variety of meditation practices within each religion and spiritual tradition. Each of these practices was originally designed to fulfill a specific soteriological goal or spiritual purpose that varied from tradition to tradition. InterSpiritual Meditation honors the goals of each tradition, though it is primarily concerned with process and method, rather than metaphysical truths and results that vary within each tradition and between individual meditators. It is a seven-step, non-sectarian, universal process that cultivates our motivation, gratitude, transformation, compassionate intention, mindful attention, meditative wisdom and dedication to service.

InterSpiritual Meditation takes advantage of one of the great opportunities of our global society. For today, the unprecedented confluence of the world's cultures has revealed a marvelous diversity of spiritual traditions, each with a precious contribution to make. In this era of global communication, commerce, and travel, people of vastly different cultures are bumping into one another with greater and greater frequency. Unlike any other time in our past, we now have the opportunity to share the deep wisdom of our traditions and practices with one another without great fear of social sanction. This InterSpiritual movement that began with early interfaith gatherings promoting 'tolerance' and 'respect,' has now evolved into the deeper and more nuanced work of InterSpirituality, that is open to a genuine experiential sharing among practitioners from diverse spiritual and secular traditions.

InterSpirituality is an open-hearted and unbiased container for contemplatives from different traditions to sit and meditate together, to enter into a deep dialogue of sound and silence, and to articulate the shared practices and experiences that are the foundations of their respective spiritual traditions. This is done not only in an attempt to understand, but to learn deeply from one another, and to create a core of spiritual intimacy based upon shared experience. Through this InterSpiritual approach, we are allowed to discover for ourselves, "the shared mystic heart beating in the center of the world's deepest spiritual traditions." In so doing, we can never again regard each other as 'the other.' We are *InterSpiritually* bound together in the shared heart-space of human religious experience. Once this happens, we are joined in compassionate concern for the welfare of all beings.

## A SEVEN-PART PROCESS

Over the past dozen years, I have worked closely with over forty leaders and authentic teachers of the Buddhist, Christian, Hindu, Jewish, Muslim, and Native American traditions. First, as a part of Father Thomas Keating's ground-breaking inter-religious retreats held at St. Benedict's Monastery in Snowmass, Colorado. Later, through the InterSpiritual programs of the Spiritual Paths Foundation which I founded in 2000 (largely in response to what I had experienced in Father Thomas' Snowmass Conference). In both venues, I had the unique opportunity of exploring many of the common themes of the world's religions from the perspectives of seasoned spiritual practitioners, and of sharing in the depths of their own meditative techniques, processes and experiences.

What I learned was quite surprising to me; for though I was well trained in the Tibetan Buddhist tradition, I found that my understanding of Buddhism and Buddhist meditation was deepened and enhanced by experiencing parallel teachings and meditations in different spiritual traditions. It became quite clear that there were shared processes found in nearly all of the traditions which made their meditations more effective, and affective as well. Thus, I began to see that these shared meditative processes might be distilled into a unique InterSpiritual practice, allowing people of different traditions to meditate together, sharing one process, while still keeping what is unique to their own traditions intact.

Therefore, this book offers a seven-part meditation process that can be practiced alone, in the company of people from the same tradition, or with people from many different traditions.

It is designed to help you develop a foundation for health, inner peace, wisdom and compassion; and its purpose is to foster these sacred qualities in group practice, bringing about a shared experience of the sacred which may bring a little more harmony into our divided world. I call it InterSpiritual Meditation because it draws together the key components of meditative processes found in many of the world's religions. Indeed, it is nothing more than a distillation of intentions and practices drawn from the ancient wisdom traditions, which it is hoped, may truly bring us together in an InterSpiritual Consciousness. What I am proposing is not a new religion or a new synthesis of religions, but a *process* through which we can celebrate the unique contributions of each spiritual tradition, being a way for us to better embrace the marvelous spiritual diversity that has been given to us. It is a non-sectarian process for developing a rich and mature personal practice, and for sharing in groups of people with diverse backgrounds.

# PART I
## MEDITATION
## & INTERSPIRITUALITY

# MEDITATION:
## PROCESS & PRACTICE

IN THE INTRODUCTION, I defined meditation as "a technique for attuning consciousness, which—depending on the individual, the technique used, and the spiritual context in which it is done—may lead to altered states of awareness (including, profound focus and tranquility), usually considered beneficial or transformative for individuals and groups." While this is a good 'starter' definition, it is neither specific enough to tell us *how* one does meditation, or broad enough to cover what I consider the greater *process* of meditation. So let's begin to look at meditation again, going back to the roots of the word itself and how it has been used in different contexts.

The most immediate ancestor of our modern word, meditation, is the Latin, *meditatio,* which in its original context, simply meant 'to ponder' or 'to reflect upon a matter'; and for a long time this was exactly what was meant by its English equivalent. But today, this is becoming one of the least common ways in which we use the word. We are far more likely to say, "I'll think about it," than to be very formal, saying, "I'll meditate on the matter." This is because meditation has come to be used in a much more specialized sense in recent years, following the counter-cultural wave of the 1960s and '70s which embraced many Hindu and Buddhist concepts and practices. As these cultural imports filtered into Western society and were translated into English, their frequent descriptions of inner quietude and tranquil breathing increasingly came to be described with the word 'meditation.' Thus, today we generally associate it with a technique leading to inner quietude, or to the state of tranquility itself. But this understanding only gives rise to new questions: Is meditation a 'technique' or a 'state of being'? Is it the reflective activity it was in the past, or the focusing technique of today?

The simple answer is—*yes . . . both . . . neither.*

The truth is that the word 'meditation' is sufficiently broad to encompass all of its uses, past and present. There is no need to nail it down with one strictly limited or limiting definition. In fact, I am much more inclined to demonstrate just how flexible the word is. After all, the Indo-European root is med, meaning 'to measure'. From this we get such seemingly disparate words as meditation and medical. For to meditate originally meant *to measure out thought,* and the original doctor was someone who did just that, carefully observing and considering the inner and outer causes of a disease. Therefore, early doctors were both 'wise counselors' and 'healers.' You see, the more we examine our definitions, the more fluid they become. For what are watching the breath in meditation and labeling thoughts, but a kind of measuring? And, in essence, is this so different from the activity of 'reflecting' or 'pondering'?

Of course, I recognize that these are clearly distinguishable meditative activities that may lead to different results, but I want us to begin to think of meditation as a process and not just one specific technique or result. We will certainly discuss different techniques, but the overarching vision of InterSpiritual Meditation requires us to take the broader perspective of process.

Let me give you a couple of examples of what I mean by meditation as *process,* and why it is important to take this perspective. Twice now I have mentioned that the word 'meditation' is often thought to encompass both a particular technique and its result. In the following example, the great Sufi master, Muhammad al-Ghazzali (1058–1111) gives a wonderfully detailed description of the meditative practice known as *zikr,* or 'remembrance,' without distinguishing between the technique and the result:

> Let your heart be in such a state that the existence or non-existence of anything is the same—that is, let there be no dichotomy of positive and negative. Then sit alone in a quiet place, free of any task or preoccupation, be it the reciting of the Qur'an, thinking about its meaning, concern over the dictates of religion, or what you have read in books—let nothing besides God enter the mind. Once you are seated in this manner, start to pronounce with your tongue, *"Allah, Allah"* keeping your thought on it.
>
> Practice this continuously and without interruption; you will reach a point when the motion of the tongue will cease, and it will appear as if the word just flows from it

spontaneously. You go on in this way until every trace of the tongue movement disappears while the heart registers the thought or the idea of the word.

As you continue with this invocation, there will come a time when the word will leave the heart completely. Only the palpable essence or reality of the name will remain, binding itself ineluctably to the heart.

Up to this point everything will have been dependent on your own conscious will; the divine bliss and enlightenment that may follow have nothing to do with your conscious will or choice. What you have done so far is to open the window, as it were. You have laid yourself exposed to what God may breathe upon you, as He has done upon his prophets and saints.

If you follow what is said above, you can be sure that the light of Truth will dawn upon your heart. At first intermittently, like flashes of lightning, it will come and go. Sometimes when it comes back it may stay longer than other times. Sometimes it may stay only briefly.[1]

You will notice that while there are clearly stages of preparation, practice, and result, the act of 'remembering,' i.e. recitation of the divine names, and the experience of 'remembrance,' are here covered by the same word—*zikr*. He has described a holistic meditation process, not simply a technique. The word 'technique' would only have applied to the practice, but not to the preparation or the result.

Another example comes from Catholic Christianity, which has long made use of meditative practices, and even the term meditation. But in the Roman Catholic Church, *meditatio* was part of a larger, three-part process that also included *oratio* and *contemplatio*.[2] In his classic book, *Open Mind, Open Heart,* Father Thomas Keating describes all three as part of the early prayer practice of *lectio divina,* or 'divine reading':

The reflective part, pondering on the words of the sacred text, was called *meditatio,* 'meditation.' The spontaneous movement of the will in response to these reflections was called *oratio,* 'affective prayer.' As these reflections and acts of will simplified, one moved on to a state of resting in the presence of God, and that is what was meant by *contemplatio,* 'contemplation.'

These three acts—discursive meditation, affective prayer and contemplation—might all take place during the same period of prayer. They were interwoven one into the other. Like the angels ascending and descending on Jacob's ladder, one's attention was expected to go up and down the ladder of consciousness. Sometimes one would praise the Lord with one's lips, sometimes with one's thoughts, sometimes with acts of will, and sometimes with the rapt attention of contemplation. Contemplation was regarded as the normal development of listening to the word of God.[3]

Now, there are two major points in what Father Thomas has written. The first is that the whole activity is conceived of as one process; one part naturally leads into another, like steps on "Jacob's ladder" which the angels may ascend and descend. The second is that he describes three distinct phases or categories of meditative activity that we will call contemplation, prayer, and meditation. Both this holistic notion of process and these three categories of meditative activity are central to the seven-part process of InterSpiritual Meditation.

In the same book, Father Keating goes on to say that in the 12th and 13th centuries, these three parts of *lectio divina* became separate and increasingly well-defined "methods of meditation" that began to appear among Benedictine and Franciscan monastics. Within a few more centuries, a definite process of "mental prayer" had emerged, giving highly specialized meanings to *meditatio, oratio,* and *contemplatio:*

As the Sixteenth Century progressed, mental prayer came to be divided into discursive meditation *[meditatio]* if thoughts predominated; affective prayer *[oratio]* if the emphasis was on acts of the will; and contemplation *[contemplatio]* if graces infused by God were predominant.[4] Discursive meditation, affective prayer, and contemplation were no longer different acts found in a single period of prayer, but distinct forms of prayer, each with its own proper aim, method and purpose.[5]

Some of you may be unfamiliar with talk of prayer as a type of meditation. This is likely because popular discussions of meditation tend to treat the two as mutually exclusive. However, I can assure you that this is not so. In more traditional circles—especially in Judaism, Christianity, and Islam—highly focused affective prayer is typically treated as a meditative activity.

You may also have noticed the contrast between the modern and traditional Christian meanings of the words 'meditation' and 'contemplation' as Father Thomas spoke of them. Clearly, the original Christian definition for contemplatio is very much what most people think of today as meditation. That is to say, meditation is now generally understood to be a state of inner quietude, while contemplation is seen as a process of deep, inner reflection. So the common understanding of both terms seems to have switched places. In this work, we will follow the modern convention and use the word contemplation only when talking about a more discursive practice.

The truth is, it is difficult to define meditation in any way that is both accurate and inclusive of the great diversity of meditation techniques available in the world's spiritual traditions. My intention is to attempt to define these three broad categories of contemplation, prayer, and meditation in such a way that they may prove useful for our general understanding, and with regard to their use in this particular book. However, as you have surely noticed, the word meditation has been (and will continue to be) used in general contexts as something inclusive of all the practices described herein, as well as a specifically defined activity.

## CONTEMPLATION, PRAYER, AND MEDITATION

In the foregoing example regarding *meditatio, oratio,* and *contemplatio,* we saw that different meditative activities may flow into and out of one another. This is similar, though not precisely parallel, to the way in which we speak about listening, reflecting, and meditating in the Buddhist tradition. The first of these is often described as 'hearing' the *dharma* or the teaching. If one has not heard the *dharma,* there will be no development on the path. The second is 'reflection' or 'contemplation,' in which one goes through the process of internalizing what one has heard. It is a deepening of knowledge, an anchoring of it in our thoughts. At this stage, one is often involved in what might be called analytical or discursive meditation. But realization of what one has heard is only achieved by 'meditating.' This is the experiential stage of the process. Notice that all three are actually forms of meditative activity: listening with focus and attention; reflecting and analyzing with the mind, attempting to achieve a thorough understanding; meditating, trying to achieve an actual experience of the concept through a spiritual practice. All of these are kinds of meditation, and one must go back and forth between them to achieve a thorough transformation of consciousness.

In the Christian description of how *lectio divina,* the reading of the scriptures traditionally led into meditation, the process followed a natural progression. First, one began by simply listening to the scriptures being read. This in itself is fairly passive; but imagine you are listening to the reading, when suddenly, a word strikes you as significant. If it were the Psalms, and you heard, "Everyday I offer you my praise and remember you in all that I do,"[6] you might feel a twinge of conscience and begin to think, "Oh how I have neglected You; would that I really remembered You 'in all that I do!' " This is the beginning of a contemplation that might become the catalyst for spontaneous prayer, "My God, don't let me lose sight of You again; how wish only to live in Your Presence!" Going one step further, imagine how that prayer of depth and profundity might reach an emotional crescendo that then might descend into the inner quietude of meditation!

This is the early Christian conception of the process. However, in time, as Father Thomas pointed out, each of these three steps developed into an extended practice of its own. Even so, the sense of process remained. In this book on InterSpiritual Meditation, the practices of contemplation, prayer, and meditation are also seen as integral to one another. However, they need not follow the specific progression described in the foregoing example. For the more these categories of meditation have grown into sovereign practices, the more they have shown themselves to be like fractals (i.e., the branch having within itself the pattern of the tree). So while one is engaged in meditation, a thought may arise that is worth pursuing in a contemplation, or which may stimulate an emotional prayer. Likewise, prayer may lead into a disciplined contemplation or a tranquil meditation. So even though the InterSpiritual Meditation process is divided into seven-parts with specific intentions to pursue, it should be understood that within each part, you may find yourself being pulled by natural inclination into one or another of these categories of meditation, all of which are legitimate activities.

Having said this, let's take a closer look at each category in more detail.

## THE PRACTICE OF PRAYER

Prayer is a form of spiritual practice with which some have difficulty, often because they are uncertain as to 'Who' is receiving that prayer. But prayer need not be thought of only in terms of a divine being who receives it; for when we are in crisis, many of us feel compelled to cry out from the depth of our being for help. 'Who' is this primal cry directed to? Why do we do it? It may be that it is simply a function of being human to 'express outward' what is felt within. Even if we don't have a distinct theological point of reference, we may still pray 'to the One Who hears' or 'to the receptive universe'; because, more than anything else, we want to send an urgent message into the infinite pool of possible help, into the deepest places of our own consciousness, hoping that our message will be received and answered in some form. It's like advertising for help on the Internet as opposed to putting a simple sign on your door. By praying into the 'Internet' of consciousness, the field of possible help is widened immeasurably.

There are also many different kinds of prayer. In a general sense, prayer is communication or communion with the receptive universal consciousness, the divine, or sometimes the personified being of one's spiritual tradition. But a specific prayer can take many forms, from invocation to petition, thanksgiving to praise, blessing to dedication, supplication to intercession, confession to repentance, contemplation to benediction. Prayer can involve silence, spontaneous speech, mantras, visualization, kneeling, bowing, gestures, offering of food and drink, the use of a rosary, chanting, music, the lighting of incense, or the precise performance of a ritual. Religious traditions have devised specific prayers to cover nearly every facet of life from the 'cradle to the grave.'

Again, our individual prayers do not have to be directed to another being or entity. Our 'praying for' does not necessary entail 'praying to.' Prayer can be a powerful psychological tool for setting our purpose and intention, for focusing our energy on an intended result: we might ask for the physical or psychological healing of ourselves and others; we might ask for help in creating better relationships with our spouse, family, friends, colleagues, or adversaries; we might ask for the wisdom, love, and compassion with which to help others; we might ask for rain to nourish our crops; we might ask for guidance in our professional lives so that we might gain the financial and material resources we need to help our family and community; we might pray that our leaders be infused with love and wisdom to forge peace between nations; we might pray for peace and tranquility in the world; or we might pray that divine love permeate the consciousness of all living beings to heal all suffering and its causes.

As you can see, prayer almost always carries with it the recognition that we as individuals do not have the power to single-handedly control our destinies, to manipulate the circumstances of our lives, or achieve our deepest aspirations. Prayer entails a confidence that there are spiritual realities that can help us forge our paths through life, so long as our purposes are aligned with the ethical precepts of our tradition.

In this way, whether prayer is directed to another being, within our self, or into the universe, we are evoking a deep personal wish that is far more profound than the mundane desires that generally run through our minds. Prayer activates the power of our essential being to actualize our most profound and benevolent aspirations for ourselves and others. The efficacy of prayer can be measured in our sense of peace, in our physical and psychological health, in our ability to achieve even the most difficult tasks, and our capacity to help comfort and heal others.


## THE PRACTICE OF CONTEMPLATION

But if prayer is an *expressive* activity, then we might look upon contemplation as a *reflective* activity. In modern parlance, as we have already noted, contemplation refers to thinking deeply, to considering something in a complete and thorough way. But, as a specific spiritual term, it also refers to a state of consciousness that lies at the border of deep conceptual thinking, sudden intuition, and pure meditational tranquility. It may be characterized by deep concentration, as well as profound inner observation, insight, analysis and non-conceptual intuition, both involving and surpassing the intellect. It is a profoundly reflective state of consciousness that can arise, for example, while sitting in silence, reading, being in nature, or engaging in art or music. Contemplation is our means of consciously traveling back and forth between the sacred and the profane, the divine and the worldly.

In my experience, it can be likened to a continuous stream flowing from the pure waters of the highest mountain snows through all manner of terrain on its way to the sea. It carries with it the sacred and profane ingredients of all the lands it has passed through. Contemplative consciousness can be non-conceptual and intuitive; it can know without thinking. It can be the conduit carrying spiritual wisdom of the sacred to the intellect. Once this experience is perceived by the intellect, it is categorized, interpreted, and expressed by words, numbers, shapes, colors, music or actions in the contemplative activity. This is the difference between ordinary contemplation and spiritual contemplation. The latter is not limited by the contracted state of awareness in which we usually operate, the 'shopping mall mentality.' Spiritual contemplation has an open connection to deeper and more profound awareness, to spiritual insights that are then unpacked in a contemplative space.

However, it is necessary to point out that contemplation is not an aimless meandering of thought, but a disciplined activity by which one explores and investigates an idea, an insight, a sacred persona, or a truth, in a thoroughgoing way, pursuing its consequences for all aspects of our lives.

## The Practice of Meditation

As we have already said, meditation can be used as an inclusive term for the whole spectrum of meditative practices, or in a specific sense having to do with bringing the mind and heart to a state of focused, calm abiding. In this specific usage, meditation is an activity that connects us to the aspect of human consciousness that has the capacity to become tranquil, one-pointed, blissful, non-conceptual, and unified with the Ultimate Reality. In Buddhism, meditation is usually described with the terms, *shamatha* and *vipashynana*. The first is a disciplined state of one-pointed focus and tranquility, with the capacity to mindfully observe and quell mental and sensory distractions. The second is the ability to harness the focused mind in the service of deep insight into the absolute nature of reality.

Generally speaking, meditation begins with a process of centering or interiorizing our awareness. Here we are no longer distracted by incessant sensory input from our eyes, ears, nose, tongue, and sense of touch, which continually draw our attention outward in a thousand different directions. Thus, we must withdraw the dominant part of our awareness away from the senses and give our mind something upon which it can fix and return its attention when it has drifted, as it almost certainly will. This 'object' of meditative focus might be the breath, a sound, a syllable, a word, an area of the body, or remembrance of an image, a concept of the divine or the sacred.

In the beginning, it is helpful to have a very simple focus. This is why we most often use the breath, for it is the most vital process of the body to which we can attach awareness with relative ease. Physical centering through breathing is extremely important for maintaining a calm, compassionate mind, and a relaxed, healthy body. It is also the most foundational of all meditative practices.

Meditation, if done properly, can bring the mind to a single focus in which there is no distraction. Meditative techniques focusing on the breath, the visualization of a sacred object, or the chanting of sacred syllables, can help us to achieve a state which allows us to rest in the present moment, without dwelling on the past or worrying about the future. These techniques can help us to become mindful our thoughts, feelings, emotions, actions, and words. They can help us to be cognizant of the infinite depth of our inner consciousness and our interrelatedness with others. They can lead to an undistracted peace of mind and tranquility. Indeed, there are many measurable benefits to these types of meditation, including, lowering blood pressure and the relief of ailments caused by stress. On a practical level, they can help us to concentrate better, allowing us to succeed in everyday tasks. And meditation, unlike many other spiritual practices, can be undertaken without accepting the beliefs of any particular religious or spiritual tradition.[7]

From an InterSpiritual perspective, we might say that prayer, contemplation, and meditation are all processes for going deeply within our own being, bringing us into the presence of an essential reality. They are meant to provide a profound spiritual realization or unity with the sacred. The world's great spiritual traditions generally teach that the intentions, methods, and fruits of prayer, contemplation, and meditation should be applied to all aspects of our personal and professional lives, to help alleviate suffering and foster health and happiness in the world.

# Religion, Spirituality
## & InterSpirituality

So how do we get from meditation to InterSpirituality? From my perspective—almost without a step. Meditation may be the most InterSpiritual practice there is; indeed, for me, it is the heart of InterSpirituality. Meditation is a state of mind in which people of all traditions can meet; for it is here that we join in the silence that Father Keating calls, "the first language of the divine."[8]

Swami Vivekananda, the great expositor of Hindu Vedanta, liked to talk about religion in scientific terms because he felt that true religion was experimentation and experience, not dogmas and theology.[9] From this perspective, meditation may be considered the 'first science' of spirituality. For it can be described and practiced without religious language or trappings of any kind. It is as accessible to the atheist as it is to the theist, though both may be forced to refine their viewpoints over time. All it requires is commitment, discipline, and a willingness to explore the inner dimensions of our being.

But what is InterSpirituality? And how does it differ from the basic ideas of religion and spirituality? To make this clear, we need to define both religion and spirituality as they are used in this book:

## Religion

Religion I take to be concerned with faith in the claims to salvation of one faith tradition or another, an aspect of which is acceptance of some form of metaphysical or supernatural reality, including perhaps an idea of heaven or nirvana. Connected with this are religious teachings or dogma, ritual, prayer, and so on.[10]

— His Holiness, the Dalai Lama

A religion is a set of beliefs about the ultimate reality of existence and human potential, about *how* and *why* we came into being, about right and wrong, freedom and destiny, happiness and responsibility, and how we must live together. These beliefs are usually based upon a transcendent experience or spiritual insight of a group or a single individual.[11] This experience or insight was then conveyed to others, who either wished to have the same experience for themselves, or to reorient their lives around the insight and teachings of the religion's founder (or founders). These early disciples, with varying degrees of spiritual illumination, then developed basic institutional structures to perpetuate the original teachings and created mutually supportive alliances with fellow followers.

But, in as much as a religion encompasses a set of beliefs, behaviors, and intentions, it is clear that we don't have to belong to an organized religion to be religious or spiritual. For each of us has a set of implicit and explicit beliefs about the nature of reality or what happens to us when we die whether we give them much thought or not. This personal 'religion' includes both experiences and reason, as well as the teachings and examples of others. These beliefs motivate our thoughts and actions, often governing our feelings about life. So whether it is our personal religion or an organized religion, religiously held beliefs condition everything we think and do, directly or indirectly, and our happiness and long-term sense of well-being are in many ways related to these beliefs.

## SPIRITUALITY

Spirituality I take to be concerned with those qualities of the human spirit—such as love and compassion, patience, tolerance, forgiveness, contentment, a sense of responsibility, a sense of harmony—which bring happiness to both self and others.[12]

— His Holiness, the Dalai Lama

Spirituality pertains to the essence or spirit of our very existence. It entails an intuitive wisdom and experiential knowledge—*gnosis, sophia, prajna, hokhmah, da'at, hikmah*—that transcends our senses and intellect.[13] It is the natural instinct that draws us to the conscious essence at the core of our being. It is the innate impulse that connects us to a higher power, a universal essence, a divine entity, the primordial state of being, or the Ultimate Reality. It is the instinctive impulse for wisdom and compassion, to be loving and altruistic. Spirituality gives an ultimate meaning and purpose to human life through which we can evolve to our greatest potential.

Many of the contemplative and meditative practices within each of the world's major religions are designed to help us experience the essence of our being, and even the essential nature of all that exists. While the names of these may be different, the initial impulse for truth is much the same.

Genuine spiritual experience is the source of the world's religions. For example, the spiritual experiences of Moses and the Hebrew people, Jesus, Muhammad, the Vedic Rishis, the Buddha, and Lao Tzu provided the foundations for Judaism, Christianity, Islam, Hinduism, Buddhism, and Taoism. Spirituality is both the source and the gateway to genuine religious experience. That is to say, spirituality is the active ingredient of religion; religion without spirituality is like a body without breath.

## INTERSPIRITUALITY

InterSpirituality is a term that we apply to the processes and experiences shared by the contemplative traditions that are nested within the world's major religions. It connotes a more nuanced approach than conventional inter-faith or inter-religious dialogues offer, that are based on 'tolerance,' 'rapprochement,' and 'respect.' InterSpirituality goes far deeper, indeed, to the very heart of the spiritual experiences that give rise to the major religions. It holds the promise of a genuine sharing of our respective spiritual experiences, and a conscious joining at the deepest levels of our being. InterSpirituality represents the next phase of understanding between people of different spiritual traditions.

One of the best descriptions of InterSpirituality I know of is that of my friend and fellow teacher, Rabbi Rami Shapiro:

> InterSpirituality does not imply the blending of religions or the ending of religious diversity. Rather, it connotes the ever-increasing spiritual creativity emerging from the meeting of and dialogue between the world's major religious traditions. This meeting both acknowledges differences between religions, and also affirms the greater unity they all

share. It is this unity that provides the common ground from which religious diversity flowers. More and more people are discovering that their respect for and love of the religion or religions of their birth need not preclude a similar respect and love for all of humanity's spiritual creativity.

It is this discovery that is fueling the growing interest in inter-religious study, practice, and lifestyle and "the recovery of the shared mystic heart beating in the center of the world's deepest spiritual traditions." InterSpirituality is a profound way of working toward the goal of global understanding, respect, and peace by elucidating the common themes, methodologies, meanings, and truths of the world's religions in full respect for the unique gifts and particularities of each tradition.[14]

## SPIRITUAL GENOMES

A useful analogy can be found in the progress of the biological sciences. While working at the Smithsonian Institution as co-director of the National Forum on BioDiversity that I learned how biology progressed from the systematic study of individual species, the ecological study of many species within an ecosystem, to the expanded study of the immense diversity of species required for the health of an ecosystem, hence every individual species in that system. Likewise, in the field of religion, we have progressed from the sectarian interest in specific religious sects, to ecumenical interest in sects within a single religion, to inter-religious dialogue about similarities and differences in religious expression, and finally to an InterSpiritual interest in the shared experiences and processes of deep prayer, contemplation, and meditation. And just as we now know that biodiversity is required for the health of each part of an eco-system, we can also see that spiritual diversity is also required for the health of each of the world's religions and their members. In this sense, religions are like families of biological species that have developed in relationship with each other. Indeed, religions have co-evolved and become resilient precisely because of their relationships with other spiritual systems.

Just as each biological species must preserve its own healthy genome (the inheritable traits of an organism) to remain viable and vibrant, so does each religion have to preserve the original genome of its founder. This genome is the founder's insight, epiphany, or relationship with a spiritual source. Just as genetic seed-banks have preserved healthy genomes of thousands of biological species, so do the most properly trained of our modern-day contemplatives need to preserve and transmit the genome of their traditions to the next generation. Thus, InterSpiritual Meditation brings together meditators from each of these traditions to help enrich, enliven, and revitalize the genome of their respective traditions. This in turn will help revitalize the original insights and intentions of each religion, and help people of all religions to celebrate diversity as they work together in unity to solve the critical challenges of our times.

### 'OPEN SOURCE' SPIRITUALITY

To use another metaphor (this time from the realm of technology), InterSpirituality can be likened to 'Open Source' spirituality. Let me explain. Over the past forty years, we have seen continual upgrades and redesigns of computer software, hardware, networks, and central operating systems. While these components are all inter-dependent, the code that controls the central operating system is the most crucial to the entire system. For example, there has been a constant struggle between the closed Microsoft model and the Open Source Unix or Linux operating systems championed by such companies as Apple and Sun Microsystems. While the Microsoft code is closed and proprietary, the Open Source code allows for collaboration between the best and brightest technical minds in the world, each of whom has expertise in a particular computer language or string of code. At the heart of the Open Source model is an ethic of mutual good, based on the premise that our self-interest is actually best served by cooperation and the sharing of the source code.

In the same way, Open Source spirituality requires the collaboration of mature and experienced meditators, scholars, and practitioners of different spiritual traditions. Joining together, they can share deep personal experiences and the subtleties of spiritual practice with one another, and sometimes actually participate in one another's rituals and practices. However, this is not to be confused with the 'supermarket' approach to spiritual development so common today, where spiritual 'shoppers' randomly choose ideas and practices that appeal to them. For there is an assumption shared by advocates of both Open Source software and Open Source spirituality; namely, that we must be experienced in the fundamentals of a single code or discipline before we can effectively manipulate, borrow, or adapt parts of it. So the practitioner of Open Source spirituality must be both solidly grounded in a tradition, and yet, profoundly open to what Father Thomas Keating calls, "the Divine Indwelling"[15] residing within, around, and beyond each person.

Open Source spirituality knows that this 'Divine Indwelling,' 'Buddha Nature,' or 'Christ Consciousness,' cannot be proprietary. Nor should the processes that led to these essential insights be considered proprietary. While the particular cultural expression of a contemplative experience may be unique, the underlying processes, or structures are universal, and thus the common property of all. This is the basic assumption of InterSpirituality. Thus, the InterSpiritual seeker attempts to deepen their understanding of specific spiritual process by learning about similar processes in other traditions. It is not that it is necessary for them to duplicate these, or even to alter their own practices, but that comparison may yield clues that will allow them to deepen and 'tweak' their own practices for greater effectiveness.

Today, many of the 'old school' leaders of the world's major religions and their various sects are still operating on the proprietary models of the past. To maintain power and credibility, they mistakenly believe that they must rigidly control the conscience of religious adherents and the information given them. They put themselves forward as gatekeepers to the experience of the sacred dimension, like pre-Internet business executives, struggling to protect their power as intermediaries in the transaction between the mundane and the sacred. They sell their services as intermediaries to the divine and as arbiters in the quest for divine approval of individual behavior. In the new era of Open Source spirituality, these 'middlemen' of proprietary spirituality will have to become skillful at helping individuals to create their own contemplative connections with an ultimate truth, even if it means adapting the code of another religion to their own personal practice.

InterSpirituality is both a reaction to this rigid proprietary attitude, and the antidote to the dis-ease that exists between so many religions today. InterSpirituality is fully aligned with the scientific fact that diversity promotes health in a population; in this case, an openness to the diversity of spiritual paths is an antidote to closed-minded dogmatism and animosity between religions. The InterSpiritual seeker knows that despite claims to the contrary from religious fundamentalists, sharing between spiritual traditions has been going on for thousands of years. For the founders and saints of each of the religions were part of a larger matrix of ideas and practices that have been flowing through the world for millennia. Only the most rigid fundamentalist fails to see the influences that spiritual programs have had on each other. Therefore, to varying degrees, each tradition is already the result of Open Source spiritual 'programming.' But even more important than this is the knowledge that some of the same concepts and processes are to be found in traditions which have had little or no contact. This strongly suggests that there is something deeper at work in the human psyche that is shared among people everywhere.

In this day and age, which has seen the emergence of the Internet and the World Wide Web (also run by Open Source systems, and based on an ethic of sharing information), it should not be surprising to see a similar spiritual paradigm emerging that respects the sacred wisdom of all the ancient traditions, and which seeks to share variations on this wisdom with everyone. The universal appeal of the World Wide Web shows us that the desire for shared information is more powerful to us as human beings than proprietary information, as does the growing desire among people everywhere to develop their own spirituality, and to make new InterSpiritual connections.

InterSpirituality strives to enable all people to experience the contemplative epiphanies of the founders, prophets, and saints; it seeks to help each of us to update our own sacred operating system so that our intellectual-emotional 'software' systems can operate in accordance with the highest potential of our being; and to make sure that our physical hardware systems are running optimally, based on a healthy, wise, and compassionate programming. As with the Internet, the genie of InterSpirituality is now out of the bottle and cannot be put back in so easily; it is time for us all to embrace a new paradigm of spiritual discourse and cooperation. As Roshi Bernie Glassman so eloquently observed:

The thing we all have in common is our diversity . . . We all wish for more. We yearn to find things that are common to all human beings, around which we can come together. But underlying that yearning is the desire for people to be the same, to be the same as us, to affirm our way of seeing things. And that's the trap . . . When we accept that everything is different we begin to see the oneness of life. Trying to find oneness without accepting those differences can take us on an endless quest that leads nowhere except to tremendous suffering for all beings.[16]

History has shown us that religious believers often wish to convert others to their own ideology. Those holding other beliefs are thus dehumanized and regarded as moral inferiors. This disease of moral, religious, spiritual, ethnic, gender, and racial superiority is the underlying cause of pogroms, holocausts, genocide, crusades, segregation, and socio-economic injustice. As Roshi Glassman reminds us, this closed approach to 'oneness' only leads to suffering. The antidote is respect and love of the marvelous diversity of life on earth, the diversity of biology, culture, language, and belief among human beings everywhere.

## A Foundation for InterSpiritual Understanding

As the peoples of the world continue to mix in increasingly diverse populations, we are exposed to a variety of cultural and spiritual strategies for happiness, as well as a proliferation of answers to our deepest questions. While this plethora of new options is exhilarating, it hasn't made the pursuit of happiness any easier. The purpose of this book is to introduce you to an InterSpiritual process of meditation that cuts across the middle of all of this diversity, or rather, gives you an option for spiritual development distilled from many different contemplative traditions.

Because meditation is an internal process, it is meant to help you become happy from the inside out, to gain insight into who you actually are and what you can become. This seven-part process of meditation can be practiced by anyone, whether you subscribe to a specific spiritual tradition or not. It is a practical process that can be used by people of various religious backgrounds, or by those who are striving for a spiritual practice without formal religious affiliation.

There is a growing trend in the western world for an integrated approach to spirituality that honors individual spiritual traditions on their own terms, but also seeks an understanding of the common wisdom and spiritual technology that is shared by these different traditions. This is part of a desire among people for a spirituality that resolves conflicts between people of different religious commitments, that embraces critical scientific thinking, and that helps support the creation of peaceful multicultural communities throughout the world.

As human beings, we naturally hope to create a spirituality that can bring peace, happiness and meaning to our lives. Thus, we are looking for an inclusive spirituality that honors personal spiritual styles and questions, and yet breaks down the imaginary barriers between religions. The healthy future of humanity and our planet seems to require the holistic integration of the spiritual, intellectual, physical, and ethical, in both our public and private lives.

In many parts of the world today, we are experiencing unprecedented religious pluralism, as well as ethnic and racial diversity. People from different spiritual backgrounds are finding themselves together in schools, professions, communities, government agencies, and in the military. As economic forces and population movements put us in closer proximity to one another, we struggle to maintain our traditions while respecting and interacting with others. In the old days, we were often united by common ethnic, racial and religious backgrounds. We shared common rituals, ethics, prayers, and spiritual beliefs. These shared beliefs and values often created a coherency of purpose. But today, this is not often the case. We share our workplace with people whose personal and inner lives we know very little about. This ignorance can create a subtle tension between us, maybe even a subtle distrust that prevents us from pursuing a common vision.

Spirituality is not usually discussed in the workplace because of fear of discomfort or disagreement. We often feel it is impolite, or an invasion of privacy to ask each other about our respective faiths. Therefore, here in America at least, Christians, Muslims, Hindus, Buddhists, Jews, and Native Americans, often live parallel lives, without sharing the depth of their beliefs and traditions with each other. This situation is also exacerbated by our division of church and state; but this division was only meant to curb invasive political control of religious and governmental institutions over each other. It was not meant to prevent healthy dialogue about how spiritual beliefs and ethical values might be actualized in everyday life, informing enlightened public policy.

With more dialogue, and greater expression of respective beliefs and values, we will find that our diversity can result in mutually held power for good in the world. By treasuring and combining our diversity, we can unleash a collective energy and imagination that is now suppressed behind the façade of proprietary beliefs. The seven-part InterSpiritual process described here provides the context for people of many different traditions to join together intentionally, to help unleash the combined spiritual potential that lies within us. In this shared contemplative process, we bring together the prayers, teachings, and practices of our respective traditions and integrate them into a common structure. We can either engage in this process alone, or with members of our families, our communities, our places of work, places of worship, and hopefully, with people who belong to different spiritual traditions. In so doing, we may begin to create a truly InterSpiritual liturgy and a new form of prayer that can include people of all faiths and beliefs.

# THE PROCESS
# OF INTERSPIRITUAL MEDITATION

BACK IN 1997, I was invited to be a part of Father Thomas Keating's famous Snowmass Conference. In the early 1980s, Father Thomas, one of the founders of the Centering Prayer movement and a former Cistercian abbot, began inviting spiritual leaders from many different religious traditions to a private retreat at St. Benedict's Monastery in Snowmass, Colorado (described in the book, *The Common Heart: An Experience of Interreligious Dialogue*). Over the course of four days, representatives of different religious traditions would sit together in meditation and then dialogue about their respective spiritual practices and experiences, often finding common ground, and more often, forming intimate and lasting friendships. That year, Father Thomas invited me to join them, to "be the Buddhist," as one of the founding members couldn't make it.[17] I didn't feel particularly qualified, but after a few deep discussions with him about my growing interest in inter-faith work, he convinced me that it would be useful for me to attend and see how it worked in the Snowmass Conference.

I felt incredibly honored. I had heard so much about the Snowmass Conference over the years. It had a reputation for doing the kind of deep contemplative work that was not to be found in other inter-faith groups, and I was not to be disappointed. Both the meditation and the dialogue were profound experiences for me. Although I had been interested in inter-faith work for a while, I really had no idea that there existed such extraordinary commonalities between the great contemplative traditions, especially among their mature practitioners. It also became clear—much to my surprise—that all of the religions represented had deep and profound practices of meditation, all aimed at developing inner peace, wisdom, and compassion.

On the morning of the second day of the retreat, we convened for a meditation before breakfast, then another meditation before beginning our morning conversation. It was during that second meditation session and the ensuing dialogue that something quite spectacular happened within me, a profound awakening that changed the course of my life. Through these meditation sessions—even though it was only the second day—I was gradually becoming aware of a kind of 'InterSpiritual Consciousness' emerging in shared time, space, and silence. And by experiencing and dialoguing about one another's distinctive practices, I found that each of us was helped to discover new depths in our own individual spiritual practices. Moreover, I began to see that the religions of the world were not isolated institutions, but interdependent phenomena within a vast spiritual eco-system. This revelation led me to envision the Spiritual Paths Foundation and the Spiritual Paths Institute as vehicles of InterSpiritual education and understanding.

It was not that I suddenly realized that all religions are the same; *they're not,* but there is something in the human spiritual consciousness that is shared by people of all traditions. This realization hit me so powerfully that I began to think: If I could just bring together great teachers—following the example of the Snowmass Conference—to dialogue and meditate together before a public program, the shared feeling would be palpable, and would surely have a profound impact on the program and all those in attendance. This would then become the true basis of an InterSpiritual understanding and peace—not just the words, the tolerance, and the commonalities, but a common experience of sharing at depth. Once people share at this level, they can no longer treat each other inhumanely on the basis of differences in religion. This was really a breakthrough for me and catalyzed me to move forward in creating the Spiritual Paths Foundation and its first InterSpiritual seminars.

Not long after, I sold my business and began devoting all my time, energy, and resources to the founding of this new organization. This gave me the space to reexamine a process of spiritual education and practice I had begun developing ten years earlier (while I was still working at the Smithsonian). In this, I proposed that all of us have predominate spiritual learning styles and fundamental spiritual questions, and that our unique spiritual paths are conditioned by these styles and questions. I hoped that the Spiritual Paths Foundation might develop programs and learning materials to help each person discern and piece together their own unique path.

In 2000, I began to seek the advice and wisdom of spiritual elders like Father Thomas, Geshe Sopa, Rabbi Zalman Schachter-Shalomi, and numerous other colleagues and friends. I also set about building a unique internet-based resource to facilitate the seeker's inquiry, and created the first offerings of the Spiritual Paths Institute, a series of InterSpiritual seminars for the public. These were to be modeled on the kind of dialogue I had witnessed as a member of Father Thomas' Snowmass Conference.

To each seminar, I invited 'exemplars' from the world's great spiritual traditions to spend several days together. In the course of these days, we meditated together, shared meals, formed friendships, and began a private dialogue that culminated in a public seminar. At the seminar, each teacher gave their own perspective on the particular spiritual theme (i.e., spiritual style or question) and later participated in a focused InterSpiritual dialogue before an audience. After the audience had heard all the speakers, they were given the opportunity to ask their specific questions of the speaker who had touched them most in a smaller group setting. In this way, we could explore themes and questions from many different spiritual perspectives and in a very personal way.

We held our first Spiritual Paths seminar on "The Way of Contemplation and Mediation" in Aspen, Colorado in July of 2002. Since then, we have held over twenty such programs in Colorado, California, New York, and British Columbia. A few of the topics of these seminars include: "The Way of the Mystic," "The Way of Faith and Devotion," "The Path of Love and Compassion," and "Living Fully: Preparing for the End of Life and Beyond." Out of the last of these seminars came the book, *Living Fully, Dying Well: Reflecting on Death to Find Your Life's Meaning,* which looked at the issues of dying and the afterlife from an integrated perspective, including science, religion, medicine, and psychology.

Today, over forty spiritual teachers representing the world's major contemplative traditions have meditated and taught together before thousands of students in Spiritual Paths programs and seminars. But even as the topics of our discussions changed from seminar to seminar, my primary interest in meditation remained. At every opportunity, I queried these teachers about the unique meditative practices of their traditions, taking notes and comparing their processes and experiences with those of the Buddhist tradition. Immediately, I was struck by remarkable similarities and began to discern a common structure or process, one that I already knew from Buddhism. Only now, I could see that it was not Buddhist at all, but a kind of universal structure of spiritual development, one that might be used to allow people of different religious commitments to share the same meditative process in a group setting.

This, I felt, was a real breakthrough. For during the Snowmass Conference, when I first became aware of the possibility of an InterSpiritual Consciousness, it was not immediately clear how this profound experience could be transmitted to others. After all, the that was a small retreat for spiritual professionals, deeply grounded in their individual religious and contemplative traditions, often longtime meditators who could easily sit down in silence together and attune to the shared consciousness created by the group. The half hour or hour that we spent in meditation together was not formal; we simply sat in silence and meditated or prayed according to the ways in which we had been taught in our traditions. With such an experienced group, it was easy to enter into the silence with the expectation of reaching similar depths, or to share a practice, knowing that the structure would be noted by each person according to its function within their own tradition.

But how was this to be done with a group that might be as diverse in experience and ability as they were in cultural backgrounds and religious commitments? The seven-part process that evolved from my dialogue with the Spiritual Paths teachers and my own meditative experiments provided the answer. Because it is a process with discernable steps and functions common to all contemplative traditions, it can be taught to a diverse group of people without interfering with individual beliefs. As everyone follows the same steps, practitioners with varying levels of experience can at least be assured that they are sharing the same ride.

Moreover, even the individual without a clearly defined spiritual path can participate with little disadvantage. For the process only asks one to appeal *within* for the accoutrements most suitable to their own journey. Thus, I had stumbled upon a direct and practical means of creating true InterSpiritual understanding, a means of sharing spiritual experience that was not dependent upon (or in conflict with) religious dogmas or specific techniques evolved within different religious traditions. It was something new, and yet, something that had been there all along—an InterSpiritual Meditation process.

## THE SEVEN-PART PROCESS

This brings us to the InterSpiritual Meditation process itself. First of all, let me say that InterSpiritual Meditation is something that can be done alone for one's own spiritual development as well as for group practice as a means of InterSpiritual sharing. Communal InterSpiritual Meditation is an evolving process that intends to honor the traditions of each participant, while at the same time, accentuating their shared methods, intentions and goals. It helps each participant to deepen their own personal spiritual path and to support the spiritual awakening of each other. Together, we engage silently in a seven-part process of meditation in which each individual participant applies his or her own spiritual understanding and practice to each step.

As I see it, the basic InterSpiritual Meditation process is like a house with seven rooms that may be decorated in any way the owner might choose. If the owner is a Tibetan Buddhist, the walls of the rooms might be painted with the colors representing the five *samskaras,* hung with iconographic *thankas* and decorated with statues of Chenrezig and the Buddha. If they are Muslim, each room might have a *mihrab*-niche showing the direction of prayer, and those same walls might be painted blue and hung with elegant textiles embroidered with beautiful Arabic calligraphy, and on the floor would be wonderful carpets for prayer.[18] That is to say, the steps of the process are generic; it is up to the individual meditator to bring everything that is of personal value.

This process can also provide an outline for exploration of the principles and practices of a variety of traditions. You might create a study-plan for yourself around these seven steps and take a week, a month or even longer to search for resources to expand and deepen your knowledge about each topic from the perspectives of multiple traditions. In this way, you can combine your experience of meditation with knowledge about the religious and secular traditions of the world.

Since this process is comprised of shared processes from different traditions, it can be used as means of sharing the meditation experience in an InterSpiritual group setting. For once the function of each of these seven interior 'rooms' is made clear, the individual practitioner can furnish them according to their own wishes and with the accoutrements of their specific tradition, even as the person next to them does the same according theirs. The process of using these rooms in a particular way is thus shared, even as it is made more effective for each practitioner by the presence of their own internal 'décor,' i.e., their own of unique teachings and practices.

Before I begin to describe the steps of the InterSpiritual Meditation process, I want to be very clear that my primary purpose is simply to create a safe container in which each practitioner has the maximum amount of freedom to pursue his or her own practice in the context of the larger process, without being hindered by that process. The goal is not to create a new religion or a new dogmatic liturgy, but to facilitate an accommodating framework wherein spiritual diversity can flourish, where participants can experience, explore, and celebrate the marvelous variety of spiritual experience nurtured by every tradition. For, in the end, InterSpirituality is about the open and creative sharing of spiritual experience, and the exploration of the nuances and subtleties available within each meditative practice.

As my own primary experience of meditation theory and practice comes from the traditions of Tibetan Buddhism, it is inevitable that the InterSpiritual process I am describing has been deeply influenced by these traditions. However, I have also been deeply influenced by Father Thomas Keating and the Snowmass Conference, as well as by the many teachers with whom I have come in contact through my own Spiritual Paths seminars. I have learned a great deal from these wonderful spiritual teachers, especially as we dialogued and shared meditations from our traditions in private, and with our students in the Spiritual Paths Institute. Therefore, the process I am describing here reflects both my experiences with Buddhist meditation and the meditations I have done with teachers of many other spiritual traditions.

Because there are variations in the foundational metaphysics of the world's traditions, there are also variations in the spiritual expectations of adherents in these traditions. And because spiritual goals vary from one tradition to the next, the specific meditative techniques are also sometimes different. It is very difficult to find a perfect InterSpiritual terminology to summarize the vast array of meditative techniques and goals found within all the world's spiritual traditions. This is because the traditions have different perspectives on the final nature of existence, the final goals of spiritual practice, as well as the capacities of human beings to understand, practice, and actualize these respective spiritual goals.[19]

Thus, InterSpiritual Meditation uses common spiritual values to create a kind of InterSpiritual liturgy that may be joined in silence, enabling us to experience the spirit or essence of our own being, even as we make the sacred ascent together. Joining in stillness, we are free from imposing our beliefs and the names of our truths on one another. Thus we are able to honor and celebrate the practices of every spiritual tradition in silent assent and acceptance. We can experience a unifying InterSpiritual consciousness emerging from the integrity of each tradition, and we can discover a profound unity within our diversity. We are free to bask in the love and compassion, abundance and strength of our shared wisdom, being of one heart.

As you examine these seven stages of the process, you will easily recognize them; for these are not only confined to religious and meditative practice, they are practical stages in accomplishing other life-goals as well. I hope you will come to see these as practical steps to be applied to all areas of your life, but especially your own spiritual practice:

STEP ONE – MOTIVATION

*"May I Be Healthy and Happy"*

In order to achieve anything significant in our lives— whether in our careers, sports, or relationships—we must have the proper motivation. Likewise, a lifelong spiritual practice also requires strong and unwavering motivation. In this first step, we establish our motivation and prayers for physical, emotional, mental, and spiritual healing, leading to sustainable happiness. (These might include our teachers, role models, traditions, family, friends, the natural environment, and even life's great challenges through which gain wisdom and compassion to help others.) To help us persevere, we begin each session by contemplating our own personal reasons and experiences that have brought us here.

## Step Two – Gratitude
### *"May I Be Grateful for Life's Many Gifts"*

There is so much for which we can be grateful: our environment that gives us life and sustains us, life's challenges that enable us to grow, to become compassionate and wise, our ancestors and loved ones, our teachers and mentors. Whenever we learn to perform a new task, we depend on the example of others to guide us. This is especially true in spiritual practice when we invoke, remember, and honor the presence of our teachers, mentors, the saints, prophets, and founders of our respective traditions, and not least, God or the sacred dimension. We visualize and invite them to join us; we pray for their help that we might help others; and we thank them for all they have done for us. In this step, we can also invoke the infinite potential that lies within our own consciousness, a potential for wisdom, compassion, and health. We invoke these with deep gratitude.

## Step Three – Transformation
### *"May I Be Transformed Into My Highest Ideal"*

In order to improve ourselves—whether professionally, in academics, athletics, ethics, in relationships, or spiritually—we must develop a clear image of that which we would like to become. Then we must be honest about our present condition, giving ourselves a personal 'reality check' with regard to our present inadequacies and the ways in which we would like to improve. We must admit that there is something wrong, something unsatisfactory in our lives, areas that we would like to improve, and make a promise to ourselves that we will strive to transform ourselves into the beings we most sincerely want to become. Without investing in debilitating guilt, we forgive ourselves (and others) for any part we (or they) might have played in our present situation. We love the wounded parts of ourselves, the negative emotions and bad habits that need healing and transformation. We renounce our attachment to the habits, desires, and behaviors that do not serve our highest ideals. Finally, we open ourselves to love, the universal healing and transformative agent for all beings everywhere. We are now ready to embark on the meditative practices required to acquire the qualities we desire and to eliminate the obstacles in our path.

### STEP FOUR – COMPASSION

*"May I Be Loving and Compassionate"*

Practically speaking, love and compassion for others are the foundation stones for our own happiness and well-being. They are the universal currency of reciprocity between all beings, and the fundamental values that lie at the heart of all spiritual traditions. At this stage in our meditation process, we allow ourselves to be infused and immersed in the presence of universal love. We radiate love and compassion to all beings, including ourselves—love that spontaneously wishes happiness for all beings, and the compassion that constantly strives to remove the causes of their suffering. We vow to dedicate our lives to this loving and compassionate intention.

### STEP FIVE – MINDFULNESS

*"May I Be Focused and Mindful Through Breathing"*

Calm, steady, and focused breathing are at the heart of many secular and spiritual techniques of meditation. When we breathe properly, we become less stressed and distracted; we are able to think more clearly, and to focus on the task at hand. Our blood-pressure drops, and our anxiety disappears. Many spiritual traditions teach deep and profound methods of breathing that balance our energies and center our consciousness deep within our being, where we are able to concentrate on our spiritual practice. In this step, we allow our consciousness to recede from our eyes, ears, nose, tongue, touch, thoughts, and emotions. As we breathe gently, our consciousness rides on the subtle breath into our heart center. This is the place that many traditions call 'the seat of the soul,' the core of our consciousness. Residing there, we may begin our own respective meditations, contemplations, and prayers. In this process, we learn to develop the capacity of 'mindfulness,' to achieve tranquil focus, and to dispassionately observe and release our incessant thoughts, emotions, habits, and memories.

Step Six – Meditation

*"May I Become Wise Through Meditation"*

Now that the garden of our mind has been carefully cultivated, we can begin to deepen and expand the scope of our meditation. Honoring the profound and marvelous diversity among the world's contemplative traditions, we silently engage in the meditation of our own tradition or choosing, opening to transcendent insight, deep tranquility, or unity with that which is sacred to us. Mindful breathing itself can remain our sole focus or may provide a foundation for our chosen meditation.

Step Seven – Dedication

*"May I Serve All Beings with*

*Compassion, Peace, and Wisdom"*

In order for our meditation to have a positive and sustainable impact on our lives, and to truly benefit others, we conclude our meditation by rededicating ourselves to serving the highest good for everyone. As we visualize our family, friends, enemies, colleagues, communities and beings throughout the world, we vow to help alleviate their suffering and bring love, peace and happiness to all. May this meditation help us to engage in the world with wisdom and compassion.

Preparation

There is an unfortunate tendency in our culture to simply 'cut to the chase.' In this case, that would mean meditating without proper preparation. People want instant results and gratification; they don't want to spend their time with the 'preliminaries' of mental training that will enable them to meditate successfully and to develop spiritually. But trying to meditate without proper preparation and expecting spiritual transformation from it is like wanting the gratification of running a marathon without the gradual training that is required to actually run 26.2 miles—more than likely, you'll tire, pull a muscle, become discouraged and stop within just a couple of miles.

Unlike many other books that focus exclusively on the techniques of meditation, this book is almost entirely about preparation and the spiritual context of meditation. The former often sing the praises of mediation as a panacea for all the ills of modern life, while at the same time, taking the technique out of the spiritual context in which it is most effective. But what is Buddhist meditation without the Buddhist teachings that allow us to examine our mind and destructive emotions? Does anyone really expect to open their eyes from meditation and suddenly be able to 'love thy neighbor'—the same neighbor who has their music too loud while you're trying to meditate? That's a lot to expect from meditation.

Mind you, I'm not saying meditation is not a powerful tool, or I wouldn't be writing a book about it. I only want to emphasize that it is a tool best used in a well-rounded spiritual context. For the teachings of a tradition have an effect on how we understand our meditation, and the meditation has an effect on how we understand the teachings. It is a reciprocal process. Thus, I have taken great pains in the development of this InterSpiritual Meditation process to emphasize the context in which we do our meditation; for this is the mysterious 'X Factor' which may make our meditation more efficacious in terms of personal transformation.

Since this is an InterSpiritual process, obviously it would make no sense to impose a single spiritual context from any specific religious tradition. Thus, I have gathered together common values, such as Motivation, Gratitude, and Transformation, as you have seen above, put them in an ascending order generally acknowledged by the traditions, and asked the meditator to contemplate these in the language and context of their own spiritual tradition or personal experience. Even if you do not happen to belong to any particular tradition, this process of contemplation and meditation can help you to find many of your own answers and insights which may begin to unfold and transform your life.

For this reason, steps One, Two, Three, Four, and Seven, fall into the category of *contemplation*—things we consider deeply, ruminate on and allow to saturate our hearts and minds, employing deep levels of reason, intuition, imagination, and reflection. This provides the context, or the space in which we do steps Five and Six, which fall into the category of *meditation,* since they entail a centering technique and a deeper level of concentration. That is to say, we embark on steps Five and Six of the InterSpiritual Meditation process having already cultivated Motivation,

Gratitude, Transformation, Compassion and Mindfulness in the garden of our consciousness. For, as I have said, Meditation is not an end in itself; it is merely one component of a larger process of spiritual unfoldment, and is deeply effected by and influential upon our daily interactions with others. Thus, we must see it holistically, and carefully cultivate a context for meditation. When we have done this and entered deeply into our meditation, we end with a Dedication, which says that we wish to activate this in our lives, to put our new-found consciousness in the service of the causes that are dearest to our hearts.

To meditate is to intentionally develop a finely honed consciousness that is tranquil, focused, refined, and open to the infinite depths (and heights) of our most profound potentiality. The seven-part process is not sufficient on its own. It can help you along the path to spiritual awakening, but it assumes that you are either engaged in a specific spiritual tradition, or that you are grounded by metaphysical and ethical beliefs, or that you are actively attempting to find a tradition or a belief system.

In Part II, I will explain each of these seven parts and show how they can work together as a process for aiding spiritual awakening within a specific tradition, among people of many traditions, or even for individuals who do not belong to any tradition. I have described them using examples that have been meaningful to me, and which have helped me to sustain and deepen my own practice. But please understand, this is not a dogmatic, unchanging process; it is an evolving experiment to which each person must bring and apply their own life experiences. It is important that you apply the wisdom of your own tradition to this process, and use personally relevant examples to motivate and guide you along the way .

This seven-part process merely provides a context for our work together, attempting to transform us and to help us engage life in an open-hearted relationship of compassion and deep sharing. If you are practicing alone, this process can become a kind of personal liturgy or ritual containing the key elements of your meditation. Each of the seven parts can be its own self-contained meditation, but together they round out a mature and comprehensive practice. As you experiment with each, you will discover the elements most meaningful to you. These will become the foundation for your own individual practice.

|   | MENTAL STATE | PRAYER | ATTRIBUTES |
|---|---|---|---|
| 1 | Motivation | *"May I Be Healthy and Happy."* | Mind<br>Body<br>Spirit |
| 2 | Gratitude | *"May I Be Grateful for Life's Many Gifts."* | Remembrance<br>Gratitude<br>Trust<br>Devotion<br>Prayer<br>Offering |
| 3 | Transformation | *"May I Be Transformed Into My Highest Ideal."* | Visualizing the Ideal<br>Self-Assessment<br>Confession<br>Remorse<br>Inward Love<br>Forgiveness<br>Surrender<br>Commitment |
| 4 | Compassion (Intention) | *"May I Be Loving and Compassionate."* | Exchange Self for Others<br>Reciprocity<br>Universal Love |
| 5 | Mindfulness (Attention) | *"May I Be Focused and Mindful Through Breathing."* | Body Position<br>Focus on Breath<br>Concentration & Attention<br>Recollection<br>Patience<br>Perseverance<br>Observation ('Mental Spy')<br>Quiescence |
| 6 | Meditation | *"May I Become Wise Through Meditation."* | Tranquil Focus<br>Insight<br>Equanimity<br>Unity<br>Absorption<br>Transcendence |
| 7 | Dedication | *"May I Serve All Beings with Compassion, Peace, and Wisdom."* | Visualize applying this in the coming day. |

This chart is a summary of the seven-part process of InterSpiritual Meditation. Parts Five and Six are 'meditative' in the sense that they entail non-conceptual, single-pointed focus through specific disciplines of attention and meditation. The other five parts are 'contemplative' because they entail a deep state of conceptual focus on one's foundational Motivation, Gratitude, Transformation, Compassion, and Dedication. Within each of these seven parts, there are additional contemplative or meditative elements to be cultivated gradually. These are the 'mental allies' for our practice. All together, they comprise an inclusive InterSpiritual meditative process.

# PART II
# THE PROCESS OF
# INTERSPIRITUAL MEDITATION

# GETTING STARTED

MEDITATION TEACHERS and experienced practitioners generally agree that it is important to establish a predictable time and place for cultivating a meditation practice. It could be a quiet place in your home or garden where you are able to sit comfortably on a cushion or chair. You might sit in front of a small table with meaningful objects or pictures and light some incense. Just before you meditate, you might choose to review your journal, this book, or the workbook to help you formulate and envision each of the seven steps in this meditation.

If sitting is difficult, you might choose to do this meditation while walking along a beach or through the woods. You might integrate it into your swimming, Yoga or Chi Gong. Wherever you choose, it is important that it is in a predictably safe environment with a minimum of distractions.

If you are sitting, you might gently close your lips and place the tip of you tongue gently at the roof of your mouth, resting it against the back of your front teeth. If you are in a chair, let both your feet rest flat on the floor. If you are seated on a cushion, cross your legs comfortably in a half-lotus position. Sit up straight, but not uncomfortably so. It is important that your body be balanced and aligned so that breath and energy can circulate freely throughout your body. Rest the palms of your hands on the top of your thighs or in your lap.

Breath gently in and out through your nose. With each in-breath, imagine calming, healing energy circulating through your lungs and throughout your body. With each out-breath, feel your muscles and nervous system relaxing from the tip of your toes to the top of your head. Bring yourself into the present moment and let all the thoughts and emotions evaporate like white clouds into a beautiful blue sky.

Try to set aside at least 20 minutes for this meditation. Generally, the contemplative steps of one, two, three, four and seven will be shorter than the meditative steps of five and six. The focus and timing for each step might vary from day to day.

As you read about each of the seven steps, make notes in your journal to help you formulate the content and focus for your personal practice. Please do not treat any of this as doctrine, but simply as a stimulus and stepping off place for creating your own practice.

# STEP ONE

## MOTIVATION

### *"May I Be Healthy and Happy"*

*In order to achieve anything significant in our lives—whether in our careers, sports, or relationships—we must have the proper motivation. Likewise, a lifelong spiritual practice also requires strong and unwavering motivation. In this first step, we establish our motivation and prayers for physical, emotional, mental, and spiritual healing, leading to sustainable happiness. To help us persevere, we begin each session by contemplating our own personal reasons and experiences that have brought us here.*

# Step One
## Motivation

MANY PEOPLE WHO HAVE TRIED to cultivate a meditation practice have endured the challenges of back-pain, distraction, boredom, and frustration. It isn't easy to sit quietly, cultivating a calm and undistracted mind. Often, it takes many months, even years, for meditation to become a natural act and to pay reliable dividends on the hours we have invested in it. It is for this reason that we must find a strong and consistent motivation to get us through the rough spots. If we allow ourselves to be discouraged at the start, we will certainly never reach the pay-off at the end. But to get there, we need to achieve a consistent and sustainable meditation practice, and this requires a sincere motivation.

When I first started to meditate, I wanted to be convinced that meditation would improve my mental and physical health, and that it would help to create happiness in my life. I was continually questioning my teachers, looking for answers and assurance from them in this regard. And while they patiently answered my questions, they also told me that I would only gain this kind of personal assurance by establishing a consistent meditation practice.

They were right. My questioning and need for certainty was just another excuse for putting my practice off until 'tomorrow.' What I really needed was to take hold of my desire for health and happiness, and use it to motivate me in my practice. After all, my teachers weren't there to *give me* an experience; they were there to *show me* the way to a place they themselves had been. All I could do was follow their instructions and see for myself whether meditation could help me achieve the health and happiness I desired.

Thus, after many stops and starts, I gradually began to gain confidence in the positive psychological and physiological effects of meditation. This confidence was based on my own experiences and observations of people I knew who had been meditating for many years. Through a kind of spiritual experimentation—something akin to scientific empirical testing and observation—I began to see clearly the causal links between my thoughts, emotions, and physiology. I started to gain an understanding of the radically inter-dependent relationship between my mind and body, how my internal states of mind affected my breathing and heart-rate, as well as my emotional and muscular stress. Still more importantly, I saw that I could take advantage of these causal links, consciously using my meditation practice to have a positive affect on my thoughts, emotions, and physiology.

This influence on the body has largely been ignored by western medicine. In treating the symptoms of illness, western doctors usually look for physical causes, and generally ignore the possible mental causes of physical disease. Therefore, it is up to us as individuals to seek out methods for creating a healthy mind, which may in turn, promote physical health.

At the heart of this kind of healing is meditation. As meditation is, generally speaking, a process for focusing, disciplining, and calming the mind, it can be practiced both in a spiritual and a secular context. In a secular context, it can lead to inner tranquility, while also helping to heal or prevent many of the psychological causes of physical illness. As a spiritual practice, it can help to center us in the essential nature of our being, and to transform our experience of the human condition, bringing it into harmony with our most profound aspirations for liberation, wisdom, and compassion. Either way, meditation helps both the spiritual and secular practitioner to achieve the goal of health and happiness. The spiritual meditator, however, is also trying to influence and transform the condition of consciousness for others well beyond this lifetime, indeed, for all eternity.

Just as the physical world is governed by laws of cause and effect, our inner world of consciousness is likewise governed by causal principles; just as the nature of external reality is colored and shaped by projections from our internal consciousness, our relative state of inner happiness is conditioned by the quality of each and every thought we have, every word we speak, and every action we carry out. Many of the world's spiritual traditions tell us that thoughts, words, and actions of peace, wisdom, and compassion create happiness, whereas, angry agitation, willful ignorance, and jealous attachment cause suffering.[20] Thus, the time-honored practices of meditation have been designed to promote internal and external health by eliminating the causes of suffering and developing the causes of happiness.

But even if we already believe in the value of meditation, generally, it is still difficult to integrate the practice of it into our daily lives; just because we have an intellectual certainty doesn't mean that we will put it into practice . . . as anyone who has made a New Year's resolution is well aware! Therefore, we must constantly fan the flames of inspiration, motivating us to reach our goal. If that goal is health and happiness, we must continually remind ourselves of the intrinsic relationship between mind and body, between goodness and mental tranquility, between mental tranquility and good physical health.

Though western medicine has been slow to take note, modern science is now beginning to confirm what ancient wisdom has long said: in order to sustain good physical health, we must also cultivate and maintain good habits of mind. Scientific studies are also demonstrating that meditation is an extremely important component of our total strategy for mental and physical health. For example, cognitive scientists associated with the Mind & Life Institute have measured the brain waves of meditators, and have charted the particular parts of the brain that are affected by meditation. Studies at the University of Wisconsin are showing that the cellular composition of the left pre-frontal cortex of the brain is changed by meditation; this is the section of the brain that corresponds to states of mental tranquility and well-being. Research by Jon Kabat-Zinn has likewise demonstrated that meditation can reduce stress, anxiety, fear, and anger; as a result, meditation is shown to relieve the symptoms of these negative emotions in the skin, heart, lungs, and stomach. To put it simply, meditation is a practical and tangible method for achieving a healthy state of mind and body.

At the beginning of each meditation session, we remind ourselves that meditation is the best thing that we can be doing for ourselves at the present moment. But in order for this statement to 'carry weight' against our habitual tendencies and lazy excuses, it must be backed-up by compelling reasons, like those I have given above. Remember, your determination and ability to persevere will depend upon the strength of those reasons.

In the following pages, I will share some of the motivational techniques I have developed and learned from various teachers over the past forty years. These are meant to stimulate you to come up with up your own personal reasons for meditation based upon your own life experiences; for just as kids eventually rebel against their parents' rules and explanations, sooner or later, we all find it necessary or convenient to reject the reasons and explanations provided to us by others. Thus, I would encourage you to write-out or journal your own reasons and motivations for meditation. This will allow you to gain greater clarity of purpose as you express what is personally meaningful to you and will also give you something to consult before you begin each session of meditation.

## FINDING YOUR OWN MOTIVATION

The lessons I learned from my teachers, as well as from my own experience, suggest that there are at least three reliable means of creating motivation: first, it is helpful to reflect on all of the unsuccessful means by which we have sought to eliminate suffering and to create happiness in the past; second, we thoroughly examine the positive reasons why we wish to meditate, and give ourselves examples of how meditation can help us to be happy; third, we remind ourselves of our ultimate purpose for this session of meditation.

As we all have different personal histories, different religious and spiritual orientations, the individual reasons that support our meditation practice and our goals for it may likewise be quite different. Nevertheless, we are all joined in having such compelling reasons and goals, and by the fact that we all share the wonderful *and lonely* burden of our own uniqueness.

Meditation techniques have been employed for thousands of years to create health and happiness in the individual. Thus, the seven parts of this InterSpiritual Meditation process are based on these traditional techniques and are intended to help you in developing and integrating your own intrinsic physical, emotional, mental, and spiritual capacities for health. Nevertheless, our overall intention should also include the development of wisdom and compassion. These are part and parcel of our fully actualized human potential, and there is no true health or happiness without them. So as we begin to dig into our own lives and explore our own personal reasons for pursuing meditation, we should remember the larger goals of wisdom and compassion, to which self-examination opens the door.

## 1. Examine and Acknowledge Your Own Suffering

The first step of InterSpiritual Meditation requires us to solidify our motivation for spiritual practice by examining and acknowledging the fundamental reality of our own human suffering. Just as we must admit that we are sick before we go to the doctor, we need to come to grips with what is unsatisfactory in our lives before we sit down to meditate. In other words, we need to come to terms with why we want to meditate. If there is nothing wrong, then why meditate? Is it just some idle exercise, something to occupy one's time, or do we hope to achieve something with it?

Meditation is something that we do because we feel the need to shift into another state of consciousness; it is a conscious response to a situation that doesn't feel quite right. Of course, there are those who may initially be interested in meditation because it is something new to them, or fashionable, but such shallow desires will not keep someone meditating for long. It is the sense of something missing, or the hope for something better that draws one to meditate seriously. Oddly enough, it is precisely this sense of something missing, and the desire for something better, that also drives everything unhealthy in our culture.

We are bombarded by pressures to buy more than we need, to eat and drink more than is good for us, and to make sex the center of our lives. Everywhere we look, we see images of actors and models in sexy clothes, pretending to have fun as they drink, as they drive expensive cars, as they lie on the beach or dance in beach houses. It's a vision of lust and leisure barely connected to our day-to-day lives, all of it promising to make us happy. The tragedy is that none of these things can make us happy. Nevertheless, we buy them with the hope that the next purchase we be the one to create a lasting contentment.

It is a seduction; desiring happiness, we have been seduced by those who promise the easiest way to get it, and the surest way to sustain it. We are told that true happiness will come from drugs, alcohol, fine foods, fitness, sex, relationships, parenthood, wealth, and luxury. The common denominator is a promise of happiness that comes from *external* things, from *outside* ourselves. It is not that these things are 'bad' and should be avoided altogether; it's just that we shouldn't be fooled into thinking that they actually have the power to make us happy.

Throughout our lives, we struggle to achieve some measure of contentment and to avoid all hints of pain and sadness, but in so doing, we habitually fail to distinguish between the causes of happiness and the causes of sadness: we think that sweets make us happy, even as they make us gain weight and give us tooth decay; we think that expensive clothes make us attractive, even as they deplete our savings and show off our insecurities; we think that wealth makes us secure, even as we become more afraid of loss and fear that we'll be taken advantage of by those who pretend to care about us; we think that sex fills our need for connection and intimacy, even as we become increasingly addicted to it and emotionally disconnected from our partners. Again, it is not that any of these things are negative in themselves; it is just that they are mistakenly confused with happiness, and thus become subject to what Alan Watts called, "the law of reversed effect."[21]

So, what does this tell us?

*We hate misery, but love its causes.*

While food, fame, beauty, drugs, wealth and sex can create moments of enjoyment and exhilaration, they do not create happiness; they are far too temporary and transient for that. Moreover, the confusion of enjoyment with happiness only leads to addiction. In trying to sustain the illusion of happiness by 'consuming' more and more of these enjoyments, we only dull and deaden their effects, drawing us into an addictive cycle which leads to physical and psychological pain and anguish. Sooner or later in life, we all have to recognize that we've been, "lookin' for love in all the wrong places," like the Johnny Lee song says.[22] We're looking outward for the causes of happiness before we ever think to look inward. Gradually, we realize that happiness is something we must bring to the world, not something that the world will bring to us. Just as God said to Abraham, "Go you forth and be a blessing." (Genesis 12:1-2) We learn that happiness must emerge from within, and that it is proportionate to our own goodness to others, and in harmony with the true nature of our existence. Creating lasting happiness will never be as easy as eating wonderful food, putting on makeup, or being popular, but at least the payoff is real and sustainable.

So, at this point, we have to come to terms with a simple and uncomfortable truth . . .

*We love happiness, but refuse to cultivate its causes.*

Our life experience tells us that every significant accomplishment requires motivation and perseverance. Without strong motivation, we cannot endure and surmount the inevitable physical and psychological obstacles to success—the pain, the self-doubt, the boredom, the distraction, and the fatigue. All successful people require motivation, whether they are small business owners, professional athletes, parents, politicians, doctors, fashion models, laborers, social workers, or teachers. It is no different for meditators. Those who are seeking a 'quick fix' and a sustaining high from meditation are going to be easily discouraged, and are likely to quit before the blissful fruits of meditation can be savored and enjoyed.

The fundamental human struggle for happiness is not new. In one way or another, the founders of all the world's religions were proposing spiritual solutions to this dilemma. Approximately 2,500 years ago,[23] the Buddha advised his students not to seek happiness in what he called "The Eight Worldly Dharmas." For if we did, he assured us, we would certainly be disappointed. These "worldly dharmas" basically boil down to the following four pairs of opposites:

*Gain & Loss:* When we seek things to make us happy, we are often frustrated in the attempt, angry when they don't, or saddened by their loss; therefore, we suffer.

*Pleasure & Pain:* When we seek happiness through sensual pleasure, our longing and attachment to the pleasure, or sadness from the pain of unfulfilled expectations inevitably leads to pain and suffering.

*Praise & Scorn:* When we seek happiness through the praise of others, this praise eventually leads to scorn and jealousy, which are the result of the ignorance that gave rise to the desire in the first place.

*Fame & Ill Repute:* When we seek happiness through fame, the examination of our most minute flaws becomes the occupation of others, and we are eventually held in ill repute because of them. (Just look at the tabloids for confirmation.)

So as we attempt to solidify our spiritual practice, it is important for each of us to bring to mind the ways in which we seek happiness on a daily basis through these 'eight worldly dharmas,' and to contemplate their inability to make us happy. When we have done this, then it is important to formally renounce these pursuits, no longer viewing them as causes of happiness, but instead, as causes of unhappiness. Following this renunciation, we are better prepared to seek the true causes of happiness, contentment, and equanimity through spiritual experience, wisdom, and realization.

## 2. Remind Yourself that Meditation Can Help You to be Happy and Healthy

Father Thomas Keating has given us a powerful motivational tool in his description of the spiritual psychology of Centering Prayer. He says, "we constantly seek happiness through our need for *power and control, esteem and affection, security and survival,*" and explains how our attachment to these false programs for happiness leads us to think that we will be happy when we have control over our environment and other people. We think we will be happy if others regard us with unqualified esteem and affection. We think we will be happy once we are assured of life-long security and survival. The fallacy of this approach to happiness, of course, is that each of these three is impossible to achieve in any permanent way. Even if they were permanently achievable, they would not cause happiness. This is a very human fantasy that fails to take into account our most basic human desires and needs for freedom and challenge. Our fundamental human ignorance is our belief that their fulfillment will make us happy. So long as we hold on to this false belief, we are simply setting ourselves up for constant disappointment, continued dissatisfaction, and misery.

Through his triad of false programs for happiness, Father Thomas has given us a key motivational tool with which to begin each meditation session. He advises us to replace these false programs for happiness with a compelling alternative: *Our happiness comes from calming our sense-driven awareness, nestling it in the divine* consciousness instead, *the sacred indwelling that resides at the very heart of our existence.* Christians, of course, call this "divine indwelling" the paracletus, the 'helper' or the spiritus sancti, the 'Holy Spirit,' which connects God with Christ and each of us in the triune Divinity. Father Thomas gently implores us to 'cuddle up' in the parental embrace of God, to be unified in the divine love that is the basis of our being. This, he explains, is the only way to become truly happy.

But this is not a purely Christian perspective. Buddhists might speak of this basic concept of internal 'divinity' or 'sacredness' as *tathagata-garbha,* or Buddha Nature. Hindus might speak of it as the place where *jiva,* the 'limited self' is united with *Atman,* the 'unlimited Self,' which is none other than *Brahman,* the 'ever-expanding' Divine. Muslim Sufis might call this state of constant awareness of God, *zikr-allah,* and the intimate presence of God within, *ruh-allah.* Jews call the 'divine indwelling,' *Shekhinah,* and the 'spirit of holiness,' *ru'ah ha-kodesh.* The Lakota Sioux speak of *Wakan-Tanka,* the 'Great Spirit.' Each of the world's great spiritual traditions offers us an ultimate source of happiness that is not caused by the material world. Each speaks of an innate capacity we all have for an insight into, or unity with the divine, sacred, or essential nature of existence by whatever name it is called.

But you don't have to belong to any one of these spiritual traditions to see the value of Father Keating's approach, for all of us cling to the illusion that happiness will come from power and control, esteem and affection, security and survival. Regardless of our background or beliefs, a thorough analysis of these motivations reveals just how certainly these things drive us into repeating patterns of unhappiness. Once we are able to see this clearly, acknowledging it as a fact, we can begin to free ourselves from the feedback loop of misery. Like a computer program that has been infected by a virus, we must be 'debugged' and cleaned out before our mental 'processor' can function properly and allow for happiness.

From a spiritual perspective, of course, our motivation is not simply the happiness of emotional stability, or even happiness for this one individual life. Our spiritual motivation might be to descend, as it were, into the depths of our consciousness for the purpose of healing the psychological wounds that are the hidden causes of our suffering and unhappiness. But this motivation need not apply to just ourselves; it may also be expressed as a hope for all beings through all eternity!

Meditation is a doorway that opens into the inner source of happiness, allowing the internally motivated causes of happiness to manifest. But in the beginning, most of us find it very difficult. When we sit down to meditate, there are endless distractions— body aches and pains, drowsiness, disturbing thoughts, doubts, bothersome noises and recollection of endless lists of things needing to get done. Even cleaning the house or doing the dishes begins to look appealing after sitting alone and meditating for ten minutes! We also find it difficult to set aside time for silence, and hard to sit alone, period. There are so many other priorities and distractions—wanted and unwanted—demanding our attention. In the face of all of these, meditation can seem like the most difficult and unreasonable thing to want to accomplish.

Again, this is why a strong motivation to meditate is so important, and why it helps to begin each meditation session by reviewing our own reasons for meditating. When we have a deep and abiding motivation, it is easier to 'stay put' in the lonely and sometimes uncomfortable silence of meditation. A strong motivation enables us to avoid distractions and to stay focused on the task at hand. If we are able to do this, we find that *loneliness* eventually dissolves into *aloneness,* and an utter simplicity absorbs the dissonant distractions into a unified wholeness. This is the testimony of countless meditators over thousands of years, and we must remember this testimony as we persevere through the early stages of our meditation practice.

## A SAMPLE CONTEMPLATIVE SESSION

Begin by making a mental inventory of your own significant life experiences. It helps to have written them ahead of time so that you can refer to them when you find it hard to make a mental review. As you create this inventory, bring up memories of happiness and sadness, joy and pain, and focus on what you did in response to these situations. Did you try to perpetuate the happiness, or the enjoyment? Did you try to run from the sadness, or protect yourself or the pain? Both are natural responses, one trying to extend something perceived as positive, and the other trying to prevent something perceived as negative. But both tend to lead to disappointment and discontent. Moments of happiness and sadness, joy and pain, are simply part of the ever-changing stream of life. There is no way to make one permanent and avoid the other. We simply learn to recognize them, cultivate their antidotes, and counteract them with the tools of meditation.

Continue looking at these memories, bringing to mind your vulnerabilities and insecurities. Look them straight in the eye. Make an honest admission to yourself of where you lack confidence or self-esteem, or where you have been less than honest with yourself and others. Think deeply about how you may have felt unworthy of love, or how your love of others was conditioned by how they looked and behaved, or what you could get from them. Make an honest assessment of all these things, and create a 'scorecard' of the quality and quantity of your own true happiness. How much of it depended on the transient and unstable world around you? How much of it depended on the approval of others? How has your behavior and response toward others been a reflection of your parent's behavior and your relationship with them? These may not be your questions, but use them to find the questions you need to ask of yourself.

Next, recall the moments of happiness that have come from selflessly helping others through genuine compassion and kindness. This is a pure happiness that arises naturally from the moment, not a puffing-up of the ego. Distinguish between the times when you gave on the condition of being repaid, and those when you gave without any thought of recompense. Reflect on the difference between selfish and selfless giving. Observe how the good results of selfish giving end when you are paid back, and how the happiness that comes from selfless giving remains with you forever.

Now think about the occasions when you have given others advice that helped them in their time of need. Contemplate the ways in which these compassionate gifts remain with you, and envision how the practice of meditation can help you achieve greater wisdom and compassion to help others. By helping others, you will achieve happiness that is more sustainable, both in this lifetime and the next.

Next, contemplate your future prognosis for happiness, honestly assessing the likelihood of your achieving happiness when your psychological world is governed by selfishness and old, unhelpful habits.

Now, bring to mind the life example and fundamental teachings of the founder of your own chosen spiritual tradition, or of a tradition that you admire. Contemplate the fundamental teachings about ethics, compassion, prayer, and meditation in this tradition. Think deeply about how these teachings, if truly and sincerely applied, could change your inner life and help you to overcome life's challenges and miseries.

When you have finished contemplating these things, distill what you feel is important to remember into a simple and clear list of reasons for meditating. Then, as you begin your meditation session, review these reasons and renew your commitment to persevere no matter how boring or painful it gets. Bring to mind the purpose of the meditation session you are about to begin and dedicate yourself to bringing your undivided attention and focus to that which you will meditate on.

Remember, through meditation, the chaos of our ordinary mind can give way to an unobstructed clarity and the most profound potential of our own consciousness. This mind of clarity is one of the most sacred aspects of our existence, an attribute of the essential nature of our being. In this meditative consciousness, there is no separation or duality between our ordinary consciousness and that which we call the greater sacred consciousness. It is through this unafflicted, unlimited consciousness that we come to realize that our true happiness is contingent on the happiness of all beings, because there is no true separation between us. We experience universal love as the imperative to work for the happiness of others. We experience compassion as the necessary condition for alleviating the suffering of others. Through this purification of consciousness, through this realization that personal happiness and universal happiness are inextricably intertwined, our motivation becomes self-evident: *to actualize love and compassion in every moment of everyday life, and to wholeheartedly support the well-being of all living beings.*

In this way, we can begin to heal the psychological wounds of a lifetime. We can overcome our need to seek the approval of others as the basis for our own self-esteem, acceptance, security, and self worth. We can accumulate a wealth of inner peace, wisdom, compassion, and contentment that will accompany us day and night, helping us to be successful in everything we do.

### 3. Remind Yourself of the Ultimate Spiritual Goal

In order for your meditation session to bear the fruits of its ultimate potential, it is vital that you plant the seed of your ultimate purpose right at the beginning. This is different from your reasons for meditating, given above, only in that it is the summation of all of those reasons; it is what they all boil down to for you. As I said before, depending on your personal history and your spiritual orientation, your ultimate purpose may be different from someone else's, even the person meditating right next to you. Nevertheless, you are joined in a shared intent and process, as well as time and space. Whatever the differences, it is important for all of us to remind ourselves of our most personal intention as we enter into each session of meditation.

The mental acuity, calm stability, balance and insight that come from meditation positively affect all areas of our lives. They accompany us when we are injured, when we are sick, and even as we face our last moments. These difficult moments become bearable, productive, and purposeful when our minds have been cultivated by meditation.

Thus, the final activity of step one—Motivation—is to remind yourself of your most profound spiritual goal. This is not the time to hold back. With humility and full cognizance of the modest realities of your present condition, give yourself permission to dream your ultimate dream and to reach for your ultimate goal. Let this great hope and aspiration take the shape of a simple prayer to the sacred power within and beyond you . . .

*"May I Be Healthy and Happy."*

*May all beings everywhere,*
*Plagued by sufferings of body and mind,*
*Obtain an ocean of happiness and joy*
*By virtue of my merits.*
*May no living creature suffer,*
*Commit evil or ever fall ill.*

*May no one be afraid or belittled,*
*With a mind weighed down by depression.*
*May the blind see forms,*
*And the deaf hear sounds.*
*May those whose bodies are worn with toil*
*Be restored on finding repose.*
*May the naked find clothing,*
*The hungry find food.*
*May the thirsty find water*
*And delicious drinks.*
*May the poor find wealth,*
*Those weak with sorrow find joy.*
*May the forlorn find hope,*
*Constant happiness and prosperity.*
*May there be timely rains*
*And bountiful harvests.*
*May all medicines be effective*
*And wholesome prayers bear fruit.*
*May all who are sick and ill*
*Quickly be freed from their ailments.*
*Whatever diseases there are in the world,*
*May they never occur again.*
*May the frightened cease to be afraid*
*And those bound be freed.*
*May the powerless find power*
*And may people think of benefiting each other.*

— Shantideva, *Bodhicharyavatara*[24]

# STEP TWO

## GRATITUDE

### *"May I Be Grateful for Life's Many Gifts"*

*There is so much for which we can be grateful: our environment that gives us life and sustains us, life's challenges that enable us to grow, to become compassionate and wise, our ancestors and loved ones, our teachers and mentors. Whenever we learn to perform a new task, we depend on the example of others to guide us. This is especially true in spiritual practice when we invoke, remember, and honor the presence of our teachers, mentors, the saints, prophets, and founders of our respective traditions, and not least, God or the sacred dimension. We visualize and invite them to join us; we pray for their help that we might help others; and we thank them for all they have done for us. In this step, we can also invoke the infinite potential that lies within our own consciousness, a potential for wisdom, compassion, and health. We invoke these with deep gratitude.*

# STEP TWO
## GRATITUDE

GRATITUDE IS THAT MARVELOUS condition that comes as a natural consequence of having brought our hearts and minds into harmony with the world. It is also an attitude that we consciously seek to cultivate in the second step of the InterSpiritual Meditation process. For gratitude is more than just a consequence of spiritual practice, it must also be there in some form from the beginning, helping us to maintain our practice. To some, this might seem like a paradox; after all, many who begin to meditate are actually seeking help with some mental or physical turmoil, or are looking for some kind of powerful transformation of consciousness. Is a person in that condition really up to feeling gratitude? I believe the answer is yes, though perhaps not yet the gratitude of completion.

Imagine you have fallen and injured yourself during a hike in the wilderness. If someone were to suddenly come across you, offering to go for help, wouldn't you feel grateful, even though the actual rescue team had not yet come? Of course you would; desperation would immediately give way to feelings of appreciation and hope: *"I am still alive . . . help is on the way . . . and I am so grateful!"* This is the kind of gratitude that must be cultivated at the beginning of our meditation practice.

First, we bring to mind the many blessings in our lives, the people, the things, and circumstances for which we can be grateful. We invoke these and make them present within and all around us. We give thanks for our precious human lives; lives of new discoveries and fulfillment; lives that have their ups and downs, uncertainties, insecurities, anxieties and fears; lives with great joy, intimate relationships, and adventure; lives in which we sometimes find as much trouble as happiness; lives that we generally take for granted. We give thanks for all of it, and ask to be blessed with the intelligence and insight to perceive life's underlying truths, so that we may truly be grateful for our challenges, as well as our easy successes.

In cultivating gratitude, we needn't focus solely on life's pleasant relationships and circumstances. In fact, it is necessary for us to include our challenges among those things for which we are grateful. For where would we be without the obstacles that challenged us to adapt, that taught us how to overcome, the parents, teachers, coaches, or bosses who challenged us to do our best? Without obstacles, without challenge, we atrophy, just as surely as muscle tissue atrophies without resistance and use. In time, we need to become grateful for the entirety of our lives, because, on reflection, it is increasingly difficult to separate the 'good' from the 'bad.' Often, that which we thought 'good' in the moment, turned out to be 'less than good' later on; and what we thought 'bad' and resented at a particular time in our life, later was found to be the source of tremendous strength, or the catalyst for great change. Perhaps some difficult circumstance has even led you to pursue spiritual practice or meditation?

As we travel life's path, we learn that no material thing, no human relationship can be the sole cause of our happiness. Happiness emerges from the inside and embraces all of life in wholeness, as a unity. Happiness does not come to us; we bring it into our lives by the way we live in relationship with everything else: the things, events, and the people that surround us . . . and the compassion we feel for them.

It may seem paradoxical at first, but selfless compassion for others is the truest route to personal happiness. So long as we are self-centered and preoccupied with ourselves exclusively, happiness will certainly elude us. As we reflect on our own life experiences, the role that compassion plays in happiness will become obvious. Therefore, along with our ordinary worldly pursuits and careers, it is vital that we dedicate our inner 'career' to the development of wisdom and compassion, and that we consider these the true measures of our wealth.

As we learn to measure personal success by the development of these inner qualities, every moment in life begins to look like an opportunity for compassionate action, opportunities for which we are grateful. Whether a moment is painful or pleasant, it is still fertile ground for inner development. Our career as contemplatives asks us to observe both painful and pleasant experiences as profound 'teachers,' instructing us in the nature of life and its wisdom. In this way, over time, our conditioned response to every moment can become one of gratitude, and we can truly be grateful for every moment that we are alive.

When we are grateful, we are led into a deeper understanding and empathy for the intricate causes of each of these moments. With gratitude, our minds are drawn into a wisdom that is fueled by a compassionate wish to help, rather than by a fearful repulsion that urges us to flee. In this sense, both the pleasant and unpleasant moments of life are equal, and we can be grateful for both.

At this point in our seven-step process, we begin to recondition our minds, proactively engendering an overarching sense of gratitude. For example, if we are going through a period of physical pain, we embrace it and thank it. We consider the possibility that the pain might be a physical echo of an unhealed emotional issue, or simply the result of inadequate physical exercise. Either way, we thank it for reminding us of the need for healing—mentally, emotionally, and physically—and of the pain that others might be feeling as well. We use our pain as a way of increasing our empathy for others. Similarly, we give thanks to the emotional hurts from unhealed relationships with others, and rededicate ourselves to healing these relationships. Without pain, it is not likely that we would ever become aware of our inner conditions that need healing. In this way, we engage in a kind of introspective experimentation, wherein we consciously engender gratitude and repel fear, even in the face of pain.

Even death can become the object of our gratitude. For without death there is no life. In each moment we carry on through the death of countless living cells in our bodies. Similarly, all of life is revolving through cycles of birth and death. Psychologically, we die to old habits and false identities as we evolve from infants to children, adolescents to adults, adults to senior citizens. Our impending death spurs us on to complete the unfinished business of our lives and to live life to its fullest. So we can be grateful for all the great and small 'deaths' that enable us to experience the full measure of our lives.

Thus, in this chapter, I want to describe six expressions of gratitude commonly found in spiritual traditions. These are: 1. Remembrance; 2. Thankfulness; 3. Trust; 4. Devotion; 5. Prayer; and 6. Offering. Now, right away, you will notice that some of these are expressions of *doing,* that is to say, expressions of gratitude through a conscious action, while others are simply expressions of *feeling*. For example, the feeling of 'thankfulness' arises naturally when we consciously 'remember' or bring to mind those persons or factors in our lives that support us in what we are doing. In this way, these expressions—when used together as part of the InterSpiritual Meditation process—help us to cultivate a deeper sense of gratitude. Nevertheless, they needn't all be practiced in every period of meditation. These six are simply offered as a means of catalyzing your own contemplative experimentation. Hopefully, in time, you will develop your own practice of gratitude within the structure of the InterSpiritual Meditation process.

## REMEMBRANCE & INVOCATION

We begin by remembering all the people, places, and events of our life that have given us comfort, happiness, and peace. We invoke the presence of all those factors that have given meaning to our lives. These might include scriptures, family and friends, teachers and spiritual exemplars, our sacred places, weddings or births, even food, medicine, or other elements of the natural world that have sustained us. We also give thanks to the very difficult experiences in our lives that have been crucibles for the deepening of our wisdom and compassion.

Remembering what we are grateful for is the key to a life of gratitude. Of course, we all feel grateful in moments of joy and relief, but to be *consciously grateful* outside of those moments is what separates thoughtful and considerate people from those who are continually taking others for granted. The latter only feel gratitude for others when they miss them, or are 'on the outs' with them.

It should be noted that our purpose here is not to 'trick' our hearts and minds into feeling happy, injecting ourselves with good memories, and suppressing negative emotions. We are simply trying to cultivate a grateful mentality and a deep appreciation for others. Our memories of what is good in our lives are like a garden that needs to be remembered and tended faithfully before it can give its yield. This is why Rabbi Zalman Schachter-Shalomi recommends that everyone participating in his spiritual eldering workshops have a wrist-*mala* of beads representing their good memories, the blessings they have received, and the things they are grateful for. In this way, all they have to do is touch a particular bead and connect with that memory![25]

In the realm of spiritual practice and psychology, this remembrance usually takes the form of an invocation. This has a very practical purpose: to immediately connect us with the highest spiritual value, God, the Ultimate Reality *(Ain Sof, Shunyata, Brahman, Allah,* etc.),[26] and to bring to mind the spiritual prophets, saints, and exemplars (Moses, Buddha, Shankara, Muhammad, etc.),[27] and the sacred qualities (receptiveness, non-attachment, equanimity, compassion, etc.) that we would like to emulate and actualize in our own lives. These are the objects of our most profound gratitude, and we appreciate them as the sources and models of our own spiritual development. Of course, this needn't be a blind or ignorant gratitude, but one that is based on profound reflection and insight. After all, how do these sacred values, exemplars, and qualities help us? We should be able to answer those questions. The more conscious we make our gratitude, the deeper it will seat itself in our daily lives.

We are imitative beings by nature; we mold and model ourselves by taking sensory impressions from everything around us. Though we are all unique individuals, with an extraordinary capacity for creativity, we all begin by learning and modeling the behavior of others. Whether we are learning to walk, to speak, to read, to make-love, to drive, to heal, to pray, or to meditate, we all have models or archetypes in our minds that we seek to emulate, often just beneath the surface of our consciousness.

Young athletes idolize sports heroes and often try to imitate them. The youth who aspires to become a doctor has often been inspired by the helpfulness and caring attitude of a wonderful physician. An aspiring pianist listens intently to the recordings of famous concert pianists. Likewise, spiritual practitioners often place symbolic representations of their highest values (pictures of the founders, saints, and teachers of their tradition) on their altars to constantly remind of them of the qualities they want to embody. Of course, many spiritual traditions eschew any visual or anthropomorphic images as attempts to confine the divine or sacred in conceptual, ego-based limitations. But even in these traditions, the highest ethical and spiritual values are often represented in words, calligraphy, or music.[28] The point is to focus on the qualities one wants to embody, not necessarily the particular manifestation.

As life-forms of this planet, our bodies are inextricably

intertwined with the natural environment. Indeed, most of the cells in our body are not even human! Our very physical being is a magnificent composite of ever-changing, interdependent elements of the whole universe, along with the living beings whose well-being is linked to ours. Therefore, our gratitude might extend to all the elements and living beings with whom we cohabitate this precious planet.

We might invoke, remember, honor and give thanks to the all-pervading presence of the divine, the unlimited sacred dimension, the presence of divine beings, the saints and founders of our respective traditions, our teachers and mentors. We invite them to join us in our meditation practice; we pray for their continued help that we might help others; and we thank them for all they have done for us. We remind ourselves of the spiritual wisdom and the practices they have taught us as we become open and receptive to the sacred within our consciousness.

For some, this invocation might imply the literal presence of these beings. For others, the invocation might only imply their virtual presence. Whether or not we conceive of the Ultimate Reality as encompassing and penetrating us, or as separate from us, our sincere invocation is a powerful reminder and grateful recognition of the profound influence the sacred can have on our state of being. This invocation also strengthens our dedication to keep this knowledge, these beings, and their teachings present, as the guiding lights or our lives. As it says in the Psalms, "I hold You above, and remember You before all that I do."[29]

Those who don't have a sense of the sacred dimension, or who don't have spiritual role models, can still invoke the capacities for goodness, wisdom, and compassion that reside within them. Whether it is a concept of the sacred, a spiritual persona, or a virtuous mental-emotional quality, we can still invoke and remember each of these with deep gratitude for their presence in our hearts and minds. Even if we don't belong to a particular religious community or have a specific spiritual belief, we can still invoke the infinite and mysterious potential that resides in the universe of our consciousness. For it can be demonstrated that consciousness extends beyond the limits of our physical body. Just as our bodies are composed of the 'stardust' of the universe, our individual consciousness is not separate from the consciousness of all life everywhere. Consciousness is individual and shared, finite and infinite, limited and unlimited. Therefore, we can open ourselves to the infinite dimensions of universal consciousness, awakening wisdom and compassion that we can put in the service of helping others.

Even as we gather together to meditate with others who hold different beliefs, who have different spiritual commitments, we still share in the act of remembrance and invocation, uniting in the understanding that each of us is connecting to the source of our highest ideals. In this way, we celebrate the diversity of our respective traditions and beliefs together, and we feel the power of their convergence; we feel the unified, creative flow of diverse spiritual energies working together, harmonizing and creating a coalescence of group consciousness, while also strengthening our individual practices.

When we gather together as a community of people with diverse religious practices and beliefs, we invoke and honor the presence of all the founders, saints, and prophets. Invocation is a deliberate psychological tool in our contemplative process and spiritual awakening. It reminds us of the people and ideals that we hold most dear. It compels us to emulate and integrate them into our own lives. It regenerates our deepest aspirations and rededicates our efforts. It sets before us the highest standards by which we measure the quality of our own existence.

### Gratitude & Giving Thanks

Once we have remembered all our sources of appreciation and inspiration, we remind ourselves of our highest ideals and those who have exemplified these ideals. Then we invoke the presence of our teachers and loved ones and ask them to be present with us. In this way, a natural gratitude begins to arise within us.

Now we take this opportunity to express our deepest thanks to the sources of these ideals, remembering all they have done for us. If we are remembering our family, friends, and mentors, the gratitude is natural, and the things for which we are grateful come easily to mind. If we are remembering and feeling gratitude to the sacred ground of all being, the giving of our thanks must be all-inclusive, touching on all the ways in which our needs have been and are being met. In the case of the founders of our spiritual traditions and our teachers, we might consider how they have passed down to us a precious lineage of teachings and spiritual experience, transmitted from teacher to student for hundreds or thousands of years. In receiving these teachings, we can be grateful for each and every link in that chain of experience.

Historically, the teachers of all our traditions faced great difficulties in preserving the teachings and scriptures that we now study. Without a doubt, these difficulties deepened their wisdom and compassion. Understanding this, we can rededicate ourselves to facing the difficulties of our own lives with gratitude. For every experience of pain, sickness, anger, or financial stress provides us with a new opportunity to enrich our lives with another level of wisdom and compassion. Just as our teachers have persevered, we too must carry on and hold our place as a link in the great chain of transmission.

## TRUST & FAITH

Having remembered that for which we are grateful, and having given thanks for the ways in which our needs have been met, our trust and faith is naturally strengthened. The very fact that that our ideals have inspired us and have delivered results—those things for which we are grateful—gives us reason to go on trusting in them. In my own life, I have observed that trust and faith are the constant companions of nearly all my actions. For each action implies a kind of faith, or a provisional trust that it will yield a certain result. Each word I use is spoken with a certain confidence that it will express my intended meaning. The act of getting married expresses a certain faith in your partner, and a confidence about the possibilities of a happy life together. Each new thing that we make or buy is produced or acquired with the faith that it will satisfy a certain need and make us happy. So faith is the hidden element in nearly everything that we do.

The principle difference in spiritual practice is that faith becomes conscious. Of course, we must not confuse faith with some kind of absolute certainty about events. Faith, as the Jewish philosopher, Martin Buber expressed it, is "holy insecurity."[30] It is that which we may not be able to prove in the world of conventional values, but which nevertheless takes hold of us and inspires us with confidence. We may not know what will actually happen, but we may know that it will be 'well,' even if difficulties befall us.

Nevertheless, when it comes to spirituality, I have foun
a faith based on reason is stronger and more affective ⌐
faith that is simply mandated by others, or which gives away all
responsibility. Reason can provide a solid foundation for faith,
a place from which to jump, to take a risk, or simply another
step. We can 'generate' faith by observing how spiritual practice
has changed the lives of others, by contemplating the teachings
of spirituality, by exploring the logical possibilities of expanded
awareness, and by practical experimentation with different forms
of spiritual practice and an examination of their results. With each
step we take in faith, we develop the confidence to take another.

## DEVOTION & COMMITMENT

Devotion is built on the foundations of faith. For our faith
leads us to devotion, or to devote ourselves fully toward a certain
end, to a particular ideal, or state of being. Therefore, devotion
is a heightened state of dedication or commitment to achieve an
intended result.

Most of us are devoted to something; it could be our partner,
our work, our art, our health, our habits, our moral code, or our
friends. As children, we are usually devoted to something that we
would like to become. It could be a superhero, a princess, a doctor,
a veterinarian, or an athlete. Often, the first thing we do when we
set these childhood goals is fantasize about how great it would be if
we actually became the 'princess' or the 'the famous athlete.'

Usually, it is a particular person who embodies and becomes the
focus of our desire. We make them into a kind of idol and devote
ourselves to becoming 'just like them.' Our devotion gives us the
determination and fortitude to gain the knowledge and to learn
the skills of that particular person. We strive to get 'straight A's,'
to perfect our appearance, or practice our free-throw shooting
for hours at a time. For to excel and actually become the ideal
we adore within us, to bring that potential into reality, requires
constant devotion and hard work. Devotion is the mental quality
that keeps us on track.

So clearly devotion is a useful psychological tool that we should
cultivate in order to pursue any goal or outcome. Unfortunately,
many of us have been hurt or let down by the object of our devotion.
Our childhood heroes fall from grace, as do our friends and lovers.

We have all heard of religious leaders misbehaving, abusing or fleecing money from their devotees. In this way, we learn that blind devotion and projecting perfection onto other human beings is a mistake. Our devotion should be realistic, conscientious, and responsible. It should never be characterized by thoughtless obedience to any individual or rigid adherence to dogma. Devotion and its associated rituals are powerful psychological tools to help us deepen our practice and cultivate our own experiences, not to enslave us in dependencies. Obviously, devotion to the wrong things or for the wrong purposes can be disastrous, so devotion should always be backed up by solid reason and sound moral judgment.

Therefore, as we build a reasonable practice of meditation, it helps if we refocus our devotion toward the goal of spiritual transformation, seeing the teachings and our teachers as guides on our life's journey, helping us to avoid destructive temptations and to persevere when the going gets tough. A strong devotion and commitment built on sound reason is one of the most powerful resources we can have in our contemplative toolbox. Therefore, at this stage, it is helpful to generate or renew one's devotion to the ideals we wish to emulate.

## PRAYER & OPENING TO HELP

With a sense of trust and commitment established, we open ourselves to the source of help and support. This is either done through a simple act of will, or by expressing a particular need or desire, planting it like a seed in the womb of the compassionate source of the universe. This latter expression is what we usually think of as prayer. Of course, not everyone is comfortable with the idea of this kind of 'petitionary' prayer. Often this is because they are skeptical about the 'recipient' of that prayer, the 'who' it is directed toward. While this is an entirely understandable point of view, it is somewhat beside the point. For prayer is a human expression that we need not feel ashamed of, even if we have doubts about who may or may not be hearing it. It is enough to have faith that the expression of the need is important in itself, and that this expression is 'received' somewhere internally, and may bring about shifts in our psycho-spiritual experience of life.

For me, prayer carries with it the vital recognition that I do not have the power as an individual to single-handedly control my destiny, to manipulate all the circumstances of my life, or even to achieve my own spiritual aspirations. It would be hubris to think that I do. So it is a necessary act of humility to declare our need for help and support. Nevertheless, our 'praying for' does not necessarily entail 'praying to' an external source. We may also call on our inner resources in the Unconscious, or the deeper layers of our being. It might simply be an intentional act of the will to be open to help and support during this period of meditation, or to utter an intentional phrase like, "May I be grateful for all the support I have received." Or, we might whisper a more personal prayer to the Compassionate Source of Help, saying, "You know how I have struggled; please sustain me and send me whatever help and support I may need during this period of spiritual practice."

In this way, whether our prayers are directed to a divine source—within or without—to the universe, or to the deepest potential within us, we are expressing a deep wish that is far more profound than the mundane desires that generally run through our minds. Prayer activates support and the power of our spiritual being to actualize our most profound and benevolent aspirations for ourselves and others.

## OFFERING & SACRIFICE

Finally, we come to the end of these six expressions of gratitude, sealing all of the previous ones with an 'offering.' This is the demonstration of our commitment, where our rubber meets the road. All of us like to think about what we *want* in our lives, how we would like our lives to be, but only a few are we willing to *pay* for it; for the decision almost always requires a sacrifice that is difficult to make. For instance, if we want to go back to school or start our own business, we may have to sacrifice the security of our current lifestyle. Even if we are not entirely happy in that lifestyle, this isn't such an easy proposition, and often, it brings up a lot of fears. Even more basic is the sacrifice we make in having children; for in doing so, we make an offering of other pursuits and pleasures, dedicating the bulk of our time, energy, and money for the long-term well-being of our families.

Both sacrifice and offering are ancient concepts with roots in religious ritual from time immemorial, but many of the early manifestations of these sacrifices run against the grain of our modern sensibilities. Like Kierkegaard, we contemplate with "fear and trembling" the consequences and morality of Abraham's willingness to sacrifice of his own son to God.[31] We wonder about the animal sacrifices of times past, about the justness of offering up *their* lives as restitution for *our* sins, or sacrificing *them* as a token of *our* commitment. Of course, these sacrifices were clearly meant to illustrate serious intentions, a willingness to take the food out of our own mouths, and to offer these precious animals to a greater cause. While these sacrifices of the past may not suit all of us so well today, the principle and function of sacrifice and offering are no less valid now than they were in the past. Just look at the examples we mentioned earlier. Do we sacrifice any less today to get the things we really want?

So, as we enter into our meditation practice, thinking of all that we are grateful for, thinking of all the help and support that we need, we are finally asked to 'anty up,' to declare our own willingness to do what it takes to achieve our goals. In the Tibetan Buddhist tradition, this often takes the form of a vividly imagined offering of our most precious material possessions, even of our own bodies for the sake of achieving our spiritual goal. This, of course, is meant to symbolize and to solidify our commitment to our spiritual goals. But the offering does not necessarily have to take this form. At this point in your practice, it may be no more than a statement of intention, a kind of IOU, saying, "I will do what it takes and make an offering of my time and energy to my meditation practice in order to reach my spiritual goals." But remember, this is just an intention; you still have to deliver if you want results. The proof will come as you persevere through all the steps of the meditation process, and tomorrow and the next day, as you carve out time and energy on a consistent basis to do the work of spiritual practice.

If you are like me, you might have initially resisted such terms as 'faith,' 'devotion,' 'prayer,' and 'sacrifice' because of negative personal experiences, or disagreeable connotations in our culture. But I hope, as you gradually develop your own personally meaningful set of spiritual beliefs and practices, you will discover a new relationship with these words and the spiritual functions they represent. Having done so myself, I now find that it is tremendously useful to focus on all six of these expressions of gratitude during the second step of the InterSpiritual Meditation process. While they needn't all be explicitly included in every session of meditation, I believe it is generally helpful to be cognizant of gratitude whenever you sit down to meditate. So as we close this section, let us make this silent vow . . .

*"May I Be Grateful for Life's Many Gifts."*

*We give thanks for our variety of skills and interests;*
*For our different ways of thinking, moving and speaking;*
*For common hardships and common hopes;*
*For this family gathered here;*
*For living together and eating together;*
*For all our good times, and not so good times;*
*For growing up and growing older;*
*For wisdom deepened by experience;*
*For rest and leisure;*
*For the privilege of work;*
*For time made precious by its passing;*
*For all that has been,*
*And all that will be;*
*For all these blessings, we give thanks.*

— Our Family Prayer[32]

# STEP THREE

## TRANSFORMATION

## *"May I Be Transformed Into My Highest Ideal"*

*In order to improve ourselves—whether professionally, in academics, athletics, ethics, in relationships, or spiritually—we must develop a clear image of that which we would like to become. Then we must be honest about our present condition, giving ourselves a personal 'reality check' with regard to our present inadequacies and the ways in which we would like to improve. We must admit that there is something wrong, something unsatisfactory in our lives, areas that we would like to improve, and make a promise to ourselves that we will strive to transform ourselves into the beings we most sincerely want to become. Without investing in debilitating guilt, we forgive ourselves (and others) for any part we (or they) might have played in our present situation. We love the wounded parts of ourselves, the negative emotions and bad habits that need healing and transformation. We renounce our attachment to the habits, desires, and behaviors that do not serve our highest ideals. Finally, we open ourselves to love, the universal healing and transformative agent for all beings everywhere. We are now ready to embark on the meditative practices required to acquire the qualities we desire and to eliminate the obstacles in our path.*

# STEP THREE
## TRANSFORMATION

THE GREAT HOPE and promise of our lives is that we may be transformed into our ideal person. Of course, this doesn't mean that we have to denigrate who we are now, or wallow in self-loathing or low self-esteem. For the power to envision our ideals is actually a reflection of the inherent strength of our inner being. It is an expression of the potential that already exists within us. Still, it is important to distinguish inspired aspirations and ideals from fantasy and delusions of grandeur. Nevertheless, belief in these ideals and our ability to manifest them in any measure, no matter how small, is our greatest ally in personal transformation.

Throughout the world's spiritual traditions, we can find many models of human 'perfection.' But it is important to remember that many of the founders and saints of these traditions began as just regular human beings, ordinary folks like us. Moreover, it should also be remembered that it was often against their own wishes that they were humbly obliged to accept their roles as perennial examples for us to emulate and follow. This humility is also a part of their example. So as we visualize the so-called extraordinary qualities of these spiritual exemplars, we must remember that these are also human qualities, which they have tempered with a beautiful humility. With this in mind, we might ask ourselves— as the popular 'WWJD' bracelets advise—"What would Jesus do?" That is to say, if we were to live according to our ideals, how would we behave? For me, the question might be, "What would the Buddha do?" And for the Muslim, "Muhammad?"

Even closer to home, we can see all around us simple acts of goodness and courage in our everyday lives. We can find the living examples of our highest ideals in our neighbors and friends, sometimes even in the headlines on the news. And not just in news stories of the Dalai Lama or Mother Teresa, but in the extraordinary acts of ordinary individuals. For instance, Joseph Campbell, the great expositor of myth, told this story in his interview with Bill

Moyers:

> One day, two policemen were driving up the Pali road [in Hawaii] when they saw, just beyond the railing that keeps the cars from rolling over [the mountain ridge], a young man preparing to jump. The police car stopped, and the policeman on the right jumped out to grab the man but caught him just as he jumped, and he was himself being pulled over when the second cop arrived in time and pulled the two of them back.
>
> Do you realize what had suddenly happened to that policeman who had given himself to death with that unknown youth? Everything else in his life had dropped off—his duty to his family, his duty to his job, his duty to his own life—all of his wishes and hopes for his lifetime had just disappeared. He was about to die.
>
> Later, a newspaper reporter asked him, "Why didn't you let go? You would have been killed." And his reported answer was, "I couldn't let go. If I had let that young man go, I couldn't have lived another day of my life."[33]

What happened in that moment to allow this police officer to overcome the law of self-preservation? Campbell characterized it in the following way: "such a psychological crisis represents the breakthrough of a metaphysical realization, which is that you and that other are one, that you are two aspects of the one life, and that your separateness is but an effect of the way we experience forms conditions of space and time. Our true reality is in our identity and unity with all life. This is a metaphysical truth which may become spontaneously realized under circumstances of crisis."[34]

In that moment, this ordinary man was transformed into an ideal, self-sacrificing being of compassion, a mystic saint who suddenly and forcefully realized, if only for that instant, the oneness of all being. That potential exists in all of us, but how do we begin to bring it from the moment of crisis into our ordinary lives? As we have already said, by first bringing the qualities that we would like to embody into our everyday awareness.

VISUALIZING THE IDEAL

Whether our ideal is embodied by a particular religious figure, a Nobel Prize winning peace activist, someone we know, or a personal composite of various people, it is helpful to visualize this person and to contemplate the qualities they possess that we would like to embody. Once we create our own vision of this ideal, as it pertains to our own lives, that mental image of our future self becomes a goal that sustains us throughout our practice. We must remember, however, that this is not just a passive fantasy about being 'someone else,' but a conscious process of cultivating those qualities that we most admire in others in our own lives.

Since childhood, we have all had our personal heroes, role models, and idols; we took them from the pages of books and comic strips; we found them in athletics and history, movies and religion. We are by nature imitative beings. Consciously or unconsciously, we have spent our lives emulating and acquiring the characteristics of the people around us; sometimes for the best, sometimes not. Mostly we do this without giving it much thought, in a fanciful, 'I wish I were like that' sort of way. In the worst cases, we take impressions of the most negative behaviors, and are so wounded by the intensity of the experience, that we take on that behavior ourselves. But what I am suggesting here is different from the former example, and hopefully a remedy for the latter. For we also have the capacity to consciously choose our models, and to adopt the characteristics which we believe will lead us toward happiness and wholeness. In so doing, we take responsibility for our lives, and are no longer driven by unconscious motivations in directions that are not helpful.

Whatever preconceived notions we may have about our ideals, it is still helpful in the beginning of this process to make a list of the qualities we most admire. For example, my own list includes the following qualities:

> *acceptance   fairness   humor   nurturing*
> *selflessness   compassion   foresight   insight*
> *optimism   simplicity   courage   forgiveness*
> *kindness   patience   sincerity   dependability*
> *generosity   love   perseverance   trustworthines*
> *detachment   gratitude   loyalty   respect*
> *wisdom   enthusiasm   honesty   mental focus*
> *self-awareness   equanimity   humility*

*non-violence   self-discipline*

Getting in touch with these qualities will help you to learn about who you want to be. So take time to explore them, thinking of examples you have seen of each, and then imagine yourself in that situation, acting in this way.

AVALOKITESHVARA

The icons and iconography developed by the world's religions depict idealized forms of the highest manifestations of spiritual consciousness. When they depict the human form, it is often an idealized expression of beauty in a particular culture. But the message is not about external beauty. Rather, this idealized beauty is symbolic of virtue and the mastery of internal mental and emotional qualities. This is the message of most (though not all) anthropomorphic (human formed) iconography. So as you look at icons of the Madonna, Moses, Jesus, the Buddha, Lao Tzu, Confucius, or Krishna, try to remember what qualities these depictions are meant to express. Or if you are looking at modern photos of Mahatma Gandhi, Dorothy Day, or Abraham Lincoln, you should remember what they stand for in your own heart and mind. For me, the anthropomorphic image that works best is that of a great *bodhisattva* of Compassion, Avalokiteshvara, who is depicted with both masculine and feminine characteristics, and often with a tear dropping from her eye upon hearing the suffering cries of innumerable beings in our world.[35]

Of course, not all icons are anthropomorphic, and not all religious traditions are encouraging of these. Nevertheless, the ideal may be just as powerfully expressed through other symbolic forms. Consider the Cross, expressing the great sacrifice of Jesus, or the profoundly beautiful Arabic calligraphy which says, *Bismillah, er-Rahman er-Rahim*, 'In the name of God, the Compassionate, the Merciful.' This calligraphic representation is not only a reminder to Muslims of God's presence, but also that "God is beautiful and loves beauty."[36] The mandalas (circular graphic depictions of sacred cosmologies, attributes of God, and spiritual practices) found across cultures throughout history are another expression of our spiritual ideals. For the *mandala* often shows the ideal arrangement of symbolic spiritual qualities within the circle of our lives.

Spiritual ideals can also be expressed through sound, movement, and particular gestures. In Tibetan Buddhism, for example, tantric practices enable all aspects of our psycho-physical being to be methodically transformed through mantras (chants of sacred syllables), mudras (symbolic hand gestures), and ritual acts, in addition to the use of visual imagery. In Christianity, the Eucharist (the sacrament of consuming the transformed bread and wine) employs what might be described as a tantric-like method for enabling devotees to take-in and embody the qualities of Christ, and perhaps even to attain or become one with Christ Consciousness.

Whatever means you use for bringing the ideal into your consciousness (and keeping it there), it is important to do it regularly, with clear and sacred intention. Use the form that suits you best, or which is in accord with your spiritual tradition, for these will always be most affective for you personally.

## HONEST SELF-ASSESSMENT

Having fixed our sights on the qualities we would like to embody, and the being we would most like to become, it is important that we honestly admit the reality of our present condition. The inability to be honest with ourselves is perhaps the single greatest obstacle to a profound, stable, and mature spiritual practice. Just as with physical and mental illness, we cannot be cured spiritually without first admitting that we are sick. Once we have been totally honest with ourselves about the reality and extent of our unhelpful behaviors, negative emotions, and of our suffering, we can commit ourselves to a cure, and apply the psychological tools needed to achieve our spiritual goals.

One example of my own honest self-assessment was brought about by the chronic back pain I had been experiencing off and on for decades. A couple of years ago, in the days leading up to a Spiritual Paths weekend retreat, I suffered an especially severe episode. As occasionally happened, I was laid up in bed for several days before I eventually 'gave in' and went for anti-inflammatory injections. The injections enabled me to be present for the weekend retreat I was leading, but afterward, the pain returned and I was back in bed. So I returned to the doctor for more injections, but they failed to give me any relief this time. Then the doctor said, I either needed an operation on my spine, or he could sever a nerve in my back. Hearing this, I had finally had enough. I realized that I had been trying to give away the responsibility for healing my pain to one doctor after the next. I realized that I had to take responsibility for my own pain and find ways to deal with it from deep within myself.

I began to think about this pain I had been suffering in a different way.

The pain was emanating from a place where my vertebrae were damaged from several ski accidents, and the medical explanation was that the broken vertebrae were putting pressure either directly on the nerves, or on tissues that surrounded the nerves. Because of this pressure, the tissues were swelling with fluids, and the swelling caused the tissues to push up on the nerves. This caused a signal to be sent to my brain that was interpreted as a 'muscle injury' surrounding the vertebrae, and the pain indicated that those muscles should not be used for fear of causing them greater injury. Yet, I knew that those particular muscles had not been injured. So the signal to my brain was a false indicator. Nevertheless, the pain persisted. So the normal medical procedure would be to stop the pressure on the nerve, which could be done through an operation, steroid injections, acupuncture, massage, cold packs, or exercises that cause a decrease in swelling.

But there was something suspicious to me about this type of cure for pain. First of all, since the vertebrae are broken all the time, it follows that there should also be pressure on the tissues and nerves all the time. But I was not in pain all of the time. Thus, it occurred to me that there were other contributing causes to the pain, which I soon recognized as emotional and psychological.

So I started to explore my pain in my meditation. As I gradually dipped down into the submerged layers of my consciousness, I came face-to-face with the negative emotions that were cooperating with my autonomic nervous system and the broken vertebrae to create pain. They were buried negative emotions of anxiety, fear, and anger. Some of these were associated with my life-situation at the time, and others were the residue of emotional traumas from an earlier period in my life.

Now, these negative emotions didn't match my preferred self-image at all! I didn't want to see myself in this way, and I certainly didn't want others to see me as under the influence of subconscious anxiety, fear, and anger. In fact, I had always prided myself on appearing calm, cool, and collected. In moments of danger, I didn't appear agitated or afraid. When others were angry or upset, I was calm and comforting. When others become emotional, I was thoughtful. These were simply conditioned responses acquired over a lifetime, beginning with the examples of my parents. But as I looked deep within, I realized that there was a hidden undercurrent of anxiety, fear, and anger, and these hidden negative conditions were making their presence felt through my back pain.

If I were truly honest with myself, I would have been able to see these things lurking beneath the surface of my calm and cool reserve in those moments. But because I was able to sublimate them in moments of external stress, I had convinced myself that they were not there at all. It was this 'lie' that had occasioned the message that had been trying to get through to me for years—a message that came in the form of back pain! So now, as I began to look closely at these emotions, almost for the first time, I saw that they were related to my work, my finances, my children, growing old, death, and the unhealed relationships in my life.

In order to get rid of the pain, I realized that I had to acknowledge and be grateful to this 'messenger' and confess my hidden anxieties, fears, and anger. This was a purely practical matter, for the pain was just too great. I couldn't even stand up! My pride could no longer stand in the way of relief. It was my pain that taught me that happiness requires a total honesty with myself. When I began to acknowledge my anxiety, fear, and anger, the pain also began to abate.

Now, my newly conditioned response to pain is immediately to say, "thank you!" even if I have to shout it through the agony. Happily, I found that this sincerely stated gratitude helps to eliminate the pain, and often the relief is immediate.

Yet the deep-seated internal causes of my external pain would not be healed without a new form of meditation, especially tailored to healing these issues. This entailed a personally crafted set of visualizations, the Buddhist meditation practices of *shamatha* and *vipashyana*, as well as bathing my inner, negative emotions in the balm love, forgiveness, and Emptiness.

Now, your own personal assessment might reveal something quite different than mine. But the important thing is to look within—*honestly*—and take note of all that is real, 'the good, the bad, and the ugly,' acknowledging them as temporary aspects of your consciousness that can be healed from the inside out. If we are to be healed, we have to admit that we are sick. If we are to be transformed, we have to know what is wrong. No one else can know *your* fears and weaknesses better than you can. So explore these negative emotions, invite them to arise in the light of your conscious awareness. Realize how they have tried to make themselves heard in your life, and even how they have controlled your life. Honestly acknowledging them is the first step in taking back conscious control and transforming yourself into your ideal being.[37]

CONFESSION

As we work to develop our practice of meditation, we learn that success doesn't only come from a well-honed technique, but from the overall quality of our lives. When we meditate, many thoughts, memories, and emotions rise to the surface of our consciousness, as you saw from my meditation on my back-pain. Often what arises is actually disturbing to our meditation. This mental agitation is the fruit of seeds planted in our consciousness by previous thoughts, actions, and words. If these were negative, then our mental state in meditation will be clouded by desire for things that will perpetuate our suffering. In other words, it is virtually impossible to cultivate a tranquil meditation practice if we are behaving badly in the rest of our life. The two are inter-dependent; good meditation requires good life habits, and a happy life depends on a contemplative attitude and meditative focus.

Therefore, in the reflective process leading up to meditation, it is vitally important that we be totally honest with ourselves about the thoughts, words, and habits that cause us to suffer. Each of us has our own unique set of negativities that we don't often recognize until we are mired in personal crisis or pain. Often, we don't confront these unless we engage in some form of psychotherapy. Unless we recognize the causes of suffering, we cannot eliminate them and be happy. In recognizing these, we should confess to ourselves that they exist, be sincerely remorseful for them, and promise not to do them again.

This is not about beating up on ourselves; it is about taking personal responsibility for the causes of our own suffering. We simply take stock and admit the things about ourselves that we don't approve of and would like to go away. We shine the light of mindfulness and love into the shadows of our Unconscious. This light of compassionate awareness reveals the negativity hiding in the dark nooks and crannies of our mind. Like the thief who runs away when discovered in the shadows, negative emotions lose some of their grip when revealed in the light of consciousness introspection.

The causes of our misery generally relate to what Buddhism refers to as "The Three Poisons." These are desire, anger, and ignorance. They are called "poisons'" because they infect our consciousness with ideas, concepts, and emotions that cause us to suffer. Like poison, they make us miserably ill. Therefore, it is important for us to make a personal inventory of the poisonous aspects of our own consciousness and clearly label them as things to be healed. This, of course, requires us to apply the antidotes: non-attachment, compassion, and wisdom.

In the Abrahamic traditions, the antidotes would entail a deep contemplative and prayerful confession, an expression of genuine remorse, and the promise to renounce these unhelpful thoughts, words, and deeds in the future. These practices are most often associated with the month leading up to the Jewish High Holidays, the Christian Lenten period, and the month of Ramadan in Islam. The preliminary practices of Buddhist meditation also employ confession as a powerful psychological tool for removing the obstacles of self-transformation.

When we use the word 'confession' in spiritual practice, we shouldn't associate it with some sort of criminal declaration. Nor should we associate it with an unhealthy feeling of guilt that paralyzes us and prevents us from making positive changes. Confession is no more than an honest admission that we have simply made a mistake, or that we have a bad habit. When we feel 'guilty,' we often feel that the very essence of our being is permanently polluted; we feel judged and condemned to a lifetime of misery. But often, we have only made simple errors in judgment and unintentional mistakes. Unproductive guilt leads to a self-loathing and self-flagellation that increases our misery and prevents the possibility of applying a cure. It prevents us from embarking on an objective analysis of ourselves that can lead to positive change and a mature, fulfilling spiritual practice.

In the context of spiritual practice, true confession implies faith or confidence in the fact that we possess an inherent capacity to be healed from within, and that the ultimate cure for suffering comes from the communion of our consciousness with that which we regard as pure and sacred. To confess is to admit that we have personal problems and faults that prevent us from becoming healthy and happy. So, at this stage of the contemplative process, we bring to mind specific examples of our words, thoughts, and actions that have harmed others and ourselves: we think of the harsh words we might have said to a friend or colleague; we recall the pain we might have inflicted on someone we didn't like; we remember the angry, jealous, or mean thoughts we may have harbored toward someone else; we contemplate how these negative qualities only lead to unending unhappiness for others and ourselves; we remember that when our mind is agitated by negative thoughts and emotions, clouded by anger, infected with envy, or drowning in greed, we are unable to calmly assess our challenges and find solutions.

All of what is brought up in these explorations needs to be 'owned' and made concrete in a confession. To simply acknowledge that we that we have problem is a step, but it is not the same as taking responsibility for it; this is what we do in confession. So, at this point, we confess the truth of what we have found out about ourselves in the privacy of our contemplation. Once we clearly realize and confess these negativities within us, then we can begin to open our hearts to genuine remorse, and can vow to eliminate them through spiritual practice.

## REMORSE

With genuine confession comes a natural feeling of remorse over our thoughts, words, and actions that have created suffering in our own lives, and in those of others. There are things that are wrong with the way we are living, and we have to do something about them. Genuine remorse is the catalyst. It is not enough to recognize a problem, nor even to admit the problem; we have to allow ourselves to feel regret and remorse over it. We cannot afford to skip over this step, jumping ahead to some immediate change in our lifestyle. That will only lead us back into the same pattern. You see, without remorse, it is only a mental process. But if we will allow the feelings of genuine regret and remorse to well-up from below, these may become the fuel for real and sustainable change.

At this point, it should be very clear that honest self-assessment, confession, and remorse are really inseparable. In honest self-assessment, we make a commitment to taking a hard look at our true feelings and motivations. When we are able to see the dirty underbelly of our lives, we need to confess what is wrong. But in confessing what is wrong, we must bring the mental process down to earth and into the ground of our experience: *Why is it wrong? How is it wrong? Who has been wronged?* When we get into the concrete examples in our own lives, we awaken the buried emotions—the regret and remorse—connected with our negative thoughts, words, and actions, even if they were unconsciously driven.

Remember, this is not about crime, guilt, and punishment, but destructive behaviors, remorse, and commitment to change. This process is about consciously creating an opportunity for transformation in our lives. If we honestly feel remorse and sorrow over our destructive behaviors, then the odds that we can stop doing them are increased in our favor. It's just basic psychology. So, at this stage of the process, it is important dredge up your own troubling personal experiences, to take a responsible inventory of your own destructive habits, thoughts, words, and actions, to contemplate the harm they have caused you and others. As you do this, allow the natural remorse to arise, feeling it with compassion for the ones who have been harmed . . . yourself included. As much as anyone else, you have been a victim and have suffered the consequences of your own negative thoughts, words, and behaviors. Sometimes the damage to others and ourselves is internal, and therefore, discounted by those who only look from without, but it is not less severe for having gone unacknowledged. Allow yourself to feel regret and remorse for the negative impact on yourself and others equally. Again, this is not about 'beating-up on yourself,' but about finding the deep justification for change, and finally facing the truth with compassion.

INWARD LOVE

There are some people in our lives that we will continue to love no matter what. But, too often, we do not see ourselves as one of these people. When we screw up, we say things like, "I hate myself when I do that!" There is always the danger of descending into a cycle of self-loathing. Yet, it makes no sense to do this to ourselves, given that we don't hate and loathe the others that we love.

When our child, parent, sibling or life partner is hurting, or has failed to achieve their goal, we might spontaneously say, "I love you." And when we experience the tender care of those who love us, our pain and suffering subside. The tensions and knots that bind us are loosened. The self-doubt and misery subside. Our confidence and energy re-emerge. This allows the process of healing to begin and we regain our strength to achieve our highest aspirations.

Indeed, love is the elixir of healing and transformation. It is the potent magic for positive change. Therefore, following our honest self-assessment and remorse for not living up to our highest ideals, we don't beat ourselves. Rather, we feel good that we can imagine a higher state of being for ourselves, ennobled by the power of our inner vision and strength to transform ourselves into our highest potential. So we replace self-doubt with confidence, and our depression with optimism, our remorse with determination, and our loathing with love—the essential force in our personal transformation.

FORGIVENESS

At this point, having taken a good hard look at ourselves, we need to cultivate a sense of forgiveness. Having honestly assessed, confessed, felt remorse over our negative emotions, actions, habits, and predispositions, and regenerated our inward love, we need to find some measure of forgiveness. Forgiveness is not a wishy-washy 'self-love,' nor is it the 'universal love' of compassion (which we will get into in the next chapter). It is what I like to call, 'applied love,' and is indispensable to our transformation.

The amazing thing about forgiveness is that it works! It is a very practical method for overcoming the power of the past in order to achieve the dreams of the future. It lays a positive foundation for moving forward with optimism in our relationships, both with ourselves and others. However, real forgiveness cannot be faked or manipulated. In order for forgiveness to work, it must be honest and sincere.

But what is forgiveness?

We might define it as a psychological attribute that offers a complete pardon for a negative thought, word, or deed. In so doing, it frees us from fear of retribution, or obligation. It acknowledges that we are 'only human,' that we are not perfect, and that we are predisposed to making mistakes. While we have an inherent capacity for sensing and reasoning-out what is 'good' and 'bad,' and what is generally positive and negative, we are not always capable, for various reasons, of doing it in a given moment.

It is helpful to remember that all of us are engaged in a life-long experiment with what makes us happy and sad, and it often takes a great deal of trial and error to figure this out. Our experiment involves both our internal thoughts and our behavior towards others. And this is as true for them as it is for ourselves. So, when we make a mistake, it is critically important that we admit it, confess it, feel remorse, forgive ourselves, and vow not to do it again, moving on with a positive attitude toward the future.

Of course, this approach also applies to our attitudes and feelings about others, people who may have done something troubling or made a mistake that affected us. In order to forgive them, it helps to put ourselves in their situation, to empathize with the conditions or their life, and to become aware of the things that have caused them to behave so destructively. This sympathetic, objective analysis helps to calm our own anger and hurt feelings, and to activate our compassion and capacity to forgive.

Forgiveness is a wonderfully humbling process. For none of us is so perfect as to have avoided a thought, word, or action that has resulted in some kind of pain or suffering. We are all only too human, and we often misstep on the way to finding our true path. Fortunately or unfortunately, we have to conduct our experiments with happiness in the laboratory of real life, learning what does and doesn't work as we go. Therefore, many spiritual traditions have prescribed asking for forgiveness on a regular basis, and have instructed us to forgive ourselves as we forgive others.

When we have gone through this process thoroughly, we are finally ready to begin molding our future in a conscious way.

SURRENDER

In some traditions, the process of transformation entails a return to our natural or essential state of being. This presupposes that beneath the covering of thoughts, emotions, memories, habits and desires, there lies a pure soul or consciousness that is waiting to be rediscovered. Often this process is one of emptying out all the attributes of our 'false self' in order to reveal and rest gently in the purity, bliss and wisdom that is the potential of all beings. This process is called by various names—, self-emptying, apophasis, via negativa, and shunyata.

Often, this entails a process of 'surrender' to a higher power, God, a divine principle, or our natural state of being. In so doing, we realize that we cannot do this job by working through the constricted lenses of our intellect, ego, and willpower. However, this approach also requires careful discernment lest we fall into the trap of blind faith in a guru or a spiritual 'middleman' who might abuse our devotion for selfish ends. Properly done, however, the surrender is often a necessary step in the process of self-actualization or transformation into our highest potential. Here we give up the fantasies and false promises of popular culture. We surrender into the magnificent possibility of being fully human, and our innate connection with the essence of all that is.

COMMITMENT

Finally, the attribute that absolutely must be present in all of these steps is 'commitment.' Here we promise to stop the specific negative behaviors that we have been contemplating, and which we have forgiven. This is not like the weak promises that we make in the moment to someone whose feelings we have hurt, promises meant to get us out of immediate trouble with someone we have offended. Rather, it is a solemn vow we swear to uphold. It is a commitment that we make to ourselves. If we break this commitment, then it is a break with our most sincere intentions. So this commitment must be very carefully and seriously made. Transformation into the person we would like to be demands nothing less than the deepest commitment.

What do we commit ourselves to? To renounce our attachment to the habits, desires, and behaviors that do not serve our highest goals.

Over the course of our lives, we have been deeply conditioned by the influences of society, our parents, the media, and our friends. Our own ignorance has also conditioned the decisions and choices we have made. Our greed for immediate gratification has led us down blind-alleys and dead-end streets. Our habits and addictive behaviors have caused us to seek happiness in all the wrong places. In order for us to be transformed into the loving, wise, and compassionate beings we would be, it is crucial that we make a commitment to renounce the negative thoughts and actions that are causing our unhappiness. Without this repudiation, we will have a hard time making room for the new thoughts and positive emotions that can set us on the right track, allowing us to make a new beginning.

Renouncing our attachment to these things does not mean that we are abandoning the world. It simply means that we are starting to see the material world for what it really is: we stop projecting false expectations on it; we stop allowing ourselves to be lured astray by its lies and false claims; we recondition ourselves to becoming active participants in the world without expecting the external world to make us happy and content. In short, we make a realistic assessment of the world and act accordingly.

When we renounce our attachment to negative thoughts and actions, we replace these with a compassionate and loving engagement in the world. Non-attachment does not entail selfish separation from the world. Rather, it is a recognition that the material objects of this world cannot be the source of lasting happiness and contentment. Therefore, the most powerful form of renunciation is active love and compassion. We commit ourselves to a life dedicated to love and compassion, to the thoughts, words, and actions that manifest these qualities.

CONCLUSION

By now, you know that meditation is only one part of a larger, unified spiritual practice, not just a one-off technique. This may even be a disappointment for some who only want to get on with some deeply profound meditation that creates immediate bliss. If you feel this way, you are not alone. Most people want to be on the fast-track to transformation and enlightenment. There are literally millions of people who continue switching from one guru to the next, from one self-help scheme to another. Innocently, they sample this spiritual tradition and that one, accumulating blessings and initiations like merit badges. They read hundreds of books and learn to pronounce the difficult names of the latest Tibetan Buddhist or Sufi master to hit town. But mature spiritual practice is not only about esoteric knowledge, exotic cultures, and it is certainly not a quick-fix; the rewards don't always come quickly.

The transformation of our thought-patterns, our ingrained habits, and our behavior is not easily accomplished. It takes preparation and work on multiple levels of our being. Some of this work may seem tedious, even unpleasant, but in my experience of working with profound teachers and practitioners from many traditions, there is no short cut. Visualizing the ideal, self-assessment, remorse, inward love, forgiveness, surrender and the commitment to change are practical steps in our transformation. These are the practices of 'real men' and 'real women!' They are necessary steps for achieving the long sought after bliss of spiritual awakening. Once we engage, there will arise occasional epiphanies that hasten our journeys, sooth our minds, and give way to levels of sustainable joy and satisfaction unmatched by the more romantic, quick-fix methods.

Thus, the final activity of Step Three—Transformation—is to remind ourselves of our most profound spiritual goals. This is not the time to hold back. With humility and full cognizance of the modest realities of your present condition, give yourself permission to dream your ultimate dream and to reach for your ultimate goal. Let this great hope and aspiration take the shape of a simple prayer to the sacred power within and beyond you.

And so as we close this section, let us make this silent commitment . . .

*"May I Be Transformed Into My Highest Ideal."*

*May you behold this—*
*I have asked to be made over;*
*May you behold this—*
*I have asked to be made over.*
A good nation I have asked to be made over.
*May you behold this—*
*I have asked to be made over;*
*May you behold this—*
*I have asked to be made over.*
A sacred nation I have asked to be made over.
*May you behold this—*
*I have asked to be made over;*
*May you behold this—*
*I have asked to be made over.*[38]

— Nicholas Black Elk

# STEP FOUR

## COMPASSION

## *"May I Be Loving and Compassionate"*

*Practically speaking, love and compassion for others are the foundation stones for our own happiness and well-being. They are the universal currency of reciprocity between all beings, and the fundamental values that lie at the heart of all spiritual traditions. At this stage in our meditation process, we allow ourselves to be infused and immersed in the presence of universal love. We radiate love and compassion to all beings, including ourselves— love that spontaneously wishes happiness for all beings, and the compassion that constantly strives to remove the causes of their suffering. We vow to dedicate our lives to this loving and compassionate intention.*

# STEP FOUR
## COMPASSION

AS A PRESBYTERIAN CHILD growing up in the mid-west, I was often confused by the dichotomous dictates given me by my church and society. On the one hand, I was taught to 'love my neighbor as myself,' to 'turn the other cheek,' and to see God as loving, kind, and beneficent.[39] On the other hand, the same God was described as judgmental, wrathful, and vindictive, demanding 'an eye for an eye, a tooth for a tooth.'[40] These seemingly contradictory moral dictums were a source of conflict within me, and a dilemma with which I struggled for the first twenty-five years of my life.

As I grew into adulthood, I witnessed how our country was wracked by the same kind of contradictions, veering back and forth between the "Great Society" and the Vietnam War, the Peace Corps and the exploitation of foreign resources, the exultation of "America the Beautiful" and the pollution of our land, water and air. While working for three governors, two of whom were presidential candidates, I came to realize that our leaders lacked the wisdom to create a just society. Like their predecessors, they continually fell back on failed policies based on the fear of new threats and the age-old desire for wealth and power. It was clear to me, even then, that these atavistic approaches would neither create world peace, nor true prosperity. There had to be another way; and with the hubris of youth, I hoped to find it myself.

This youthful determination, along with other fortuitous circumstances, led me to the Dalai Lama, who in turn introduced me to Geshe Lhundup Sopa with whom I continued my studies. With Geshe Sopa, one of the most revered Tibetan scholar-practitioners of his generation, I hoped to find a resolution to this grand dilemma that I could apply in the real world. You see, I was really a 'show me' kind of guy in those days, and if I was actually going to 'love my neighbor as myself' and 'turn the other cheek,' I needed to be convinced that it was practical to do so. I needed to be given a compelling reason. I also had to feel a genuine compulsion to act. It's not that it didn't seem like a good idea; it's just that I didn't want to do it simply because someone had told me it was 'the right thing to do.' I had to have a good reason for doing it, and I had to 'feel like doing it.' It wasn't enough that Jesus had said it; I had to learn to do it myself—albeit, Buddhist-style—through a combination of real life experience and intellectual reasoning.

Even as I sought answers to alleviate my skepticism, I remained inspired by my first conversation with the Dalai Lama in 1970. For when I asked him if he was angry at the Chinese for destroying his culture and killing his people, he said: "No—I am deeply saddened by what has happened, but I am not angry at the Chinese. I have compassion for them because they are generating very bad *karma* for themselves for which they will be suffering in the future." This answer astounded me. I had never heard a leader speak with such wisdom and equanimity in the face of his own tragedy.

Another example that moved me deeply came from a Tibetan nun. She had been imprisoned and beaten by the Chinese for many years and had suffered horribly at the hands of her captors. After escaping to India, she was asked what scared her most during her captivity. She said, "I was most afraid that I would loose my compassion for my captors as they beat me."

While these examples inspired me, I still doubted if I could ever feel them for myself.

After five years of study with Geshe Sopa, I began my Ph.D. thesis on *The Perfection of Wisdom Sutras* and the 'Great Compassion' of Buddhism. To conduct my research, I received a Fulbright Fellowship to study in India, where I took up residence, first in the Indian holy city of Varanasi, then at Sera Buddhist Monastery near Bylakuppe, in southern India. The monks at Sera were refugees from the Chinese invasion of Tibet, and yet, even in their difficult circumstances and extreme poverty, they were the most friendly, cheerful, and generous people I had ever met. Their monastic education entailed a rigorous combination of intellectual training and spiritual practice. In this way, they became masters of both the rationale for, and the practice of, love and compassion, devoting their lives to cultivating the wisdom required to help others.

## Love, Compassion & Great Compassion

One of my first questions to my Buddhist teachers was this:

"What is the difference between love and compassion?" The answer I got was this: "Love is the sincere wish for the happiness of another being. Compassion is the sincere intention to remove the causes of their suffering. Great Compassion is the vow to become enlightened in order to liberate all beings from suffering." In this, the goal of these Buddhist monks seemed to resonate with the ones Jesus had laid out for us with, "love your neighbor as yourself," and "do unto others as your would have them do unto you."

The longer I lived and studied with these monks, the more I began to realize how trivial all the other goals in life were when compared with the development of Great Compassion. Why should we strive for anything less than an end to suffering for all beings? How else could happiness be achieved? And yet, even as I was beginning to generate the feeling and aesthetic of compassion, my skeptical mind kept holding me back. I still needed to be armed with 'reasons' to compel me whole-heartedly to take the Bodhisattva Vow, the vow of Great Compassion.

### SELFISH & SELFLESS COMPASSION

From a purely selfish point of view, I wondered about the personal payoff for compassion—after all, what would it do for me? So I began a series of thought experiments, the first of which followed this logic:

From a purely practical standpoint, we all know that we feel happier and more secure when we are liked by others. Likewise, we know that we gain the esteem of others and their affection when we do something good for them, without making any demands or stipulating a repayment. Additionally, we also know that when someone agrees to receive a gift, they will most likely feel compelled to return the kindness; for the responsibility of reciprocity is hard-wired in the human conscience. Indeed, this hard-wired sense of reciprocity might even be seen as a biologically determined basis for altruism. Although some people might be able to suppress the compulsion to return a kindness, they generally want to give in return, if only to compel the other to give something back again.[41] This is the mundane law of reciprocity that is quite common in everyday life.

Now, somewhere inside, we know that this 'return' is necessary for our survival; for none of us can make it on our own when times are tough. We have to be able to depend on one another, and we like to know just who it is we can really depend on in those circumstances. So, for 'insurance'—both consciously and unconsciously—we create more or less reliable networks of reciprocity among our acquaintances, and in our local communities. We engage in limited forms of generosity, trusting in the law of reciprocity, hoping somewhere inside that—to the extent that we are good to others—they may feel obligated to be good to us.

By my own pragmatic, American logic, this is how I was interpreting the Buddhist teaching of compassion. Even in the face of teachings to the contrary, I thought, this must be what they are really trying to get at! So I began to regard it as the only hope for world peace and happiness; after all, the old-school 'an eye for an eye,' and 'speak softly and carry a big stick' approaches to peace certainly hadn't worked. Perhaps a compassion based on mutual self-interest was really the answer.[42]

In some ways, I thought perhaps this was part of the positive karmic relationship of cause and effect that my Buddhist teachers were trying to get through to me; that our intention to help others is connected to their intention to help us. As our altruism extends to more and more people, there will be more and more people who will have this feeling for us. As we do more for them, they will do more for us. For example, hadn't Mother Teresa's compassionate mission for the poor compelled people throughout the world to revere her. Wherever she went, she was showered with praise and donations for her work. She was held in esteem by countless millions of people. If she were threatened, those people would have come to her rescue. In other words, her personal well-being was assured by people everywhere. If she were homeless or destitute, these complete strangers would come to her rescue.[43]

Using this logic, I tried to begin each day in the monastery with the intention to be kind to every person I would meet that day. Before going to sleep at night, I tried to develop the intention to remain in a compassionate state, even in my dreams. If, like Mother Teresa, I exemplified compassion, people would naturally feel confident that I was working for their benefit. Thus, their confidence in me would engender trust, and this trust would then open up a magnificent array of opportunities and support for me, personally. Indeed, I speculated that the effect might even begin to snowball, thus increasing the number of people who might wish to reciprocate exponentially, thus increasing my own happiness, security, and well-being a thousand-fold!

But even as I carried out this little experiment, I was told by my teachers that trying to take advantage of love and compassion, attempting to milk their benefits in a self-serving way, simply wouldn't work: the Great Compassion is selfless. At the moment of performing a compassionate act, one can have no hope or thought of repayment. The compassion must be pure and spontaneous. The subtle causality of true compassion requires—at the very least—the intention to be pure of self-interest. That is to say, the subtle hope for recompense sours the milk of compassion. For, according to Buddhism, a compassion which hopes for reward is based on desire, and an act based on desire tends to create more desire. When that desire is finally disappointed—as sooner or later it surely will be—this disappointment will cause suffering. Thus, the hope for return is just a set-up for more suffering.

This little oversight was the flaw in my pragmatic logic. It was not that there wasn't a certain truth and efficacy in pursuing the instinct and benefits of mutual self-interest, but that it is a poor scheme for achieving happiness. Increasing the probabilities for survival and moments of enjoyment derived from reciprocated generosity is simply not the same as thriving and living happily. These are conditions that are generated from within, and which must side-step the pitfalls created by self-interest. Thus, Buddhist training in the Great Compassion requires that we learn to catch ourselves when we hope for a return, as I certainly was!

Over time, through my study of the traditional Buddhist texts, and in my studies with the senior monks, I became convinced that Great Compassion could not be achieved if I was only trying to generate it for my own happiness. Instead, I began to attempt a purely altruistic wish, exclusively focused on the well-being of others. For according to the Buddhist formulation, my own personal happiness could only be achieved—paradoxically enough—by taking my self out of the equation!

When I began to seriously consider the implications of this type of intention—to help all beings remove the causes of their suffering—I seriously doubted my capacity to succeed. This feeling was in complete contrast with my former confidence about 'selfish compassion.' Even today, after nearly forty years of practice, I am still humbled by the profundity of the Great Compassion, realizing just how far I am from this achieving this goal.

In thinking of it, I am reminded of the awe-inspiring example of Jesus Christ who, we are taught, loved us so much that he sacrificed his own life so that we might live.[44] He showed us that his love and his connection with the Divine were so complete that he would give his own life to provide an example to others. And if we followed his example of love, sacrificing the self for the sake of compassion—though not necessarily in the same manner—our own sins would be absolved.

In Buddhism, another such example is found in the story of Asanga, who spent decades in solitary meditation in order to come face-to-face with Maitreya, the Buddha of the future:

> *As Asanga neared the end of his capacity to persevere, he wandered out of his cave and discovered a dying dog lying on the path in front of him. The dog was emaciated, bleeding, and surely nothing could save its life. Nevertheless, Asanga knelt down to examine its wounds and saw that maggots were eating away at the dog's decaying flesh. Hoping to heal the open wound, Asanga realized that he would have to remove the maggots. But if he did so with his hands, he ran the risk of endangering the maggots' lives as well. So he lowered his face to the wound and began to remove the maggots one-by-one with his tongue! In that instant, the image of the dog was replaced by the body of the Buddha, Maitreya. In the excitement of the moment, Asanga lifted Maitreya into the air and placed him on his shoulders and walked to the village. But as he walked along the path, the villagers only saw the dying dog lying across his shoulders.[45]*

The example of Jesus Christ on the Cross, and this story of Asanga, both illustrate the utter profundity and sublime magnificence of Great Compassion, providing us with strong images of the selfless giving that is the highest of all human aspirations.

## Limited & Limitless Love

When we use the words love and compassion in everyday conversation, we automatically assume that everyone understands what we are talking about. But love and compassion have many different definitions and connotations. In the InterSpiritual Meditation process, we are trying to evoke and talk about the deepest and most profound love and compassion. This is not a love that is limited by attraction, or even by deep affection; it isn't conditioned by how a person looks, thinks, talks, or acts, or even whether we like them or not. It is love without limits.

There is a profound difference between universal, or divine love and compassion and our ordinary use of these words. Generally, when we love someone, we want what we think is best for them, or what they think is best for themselves. This usually pertains to things like material possessions, success, popularity, financial security, and joy. This love and compassion also implies a deep empathy and concern for another person's safety, as well as their physical and emotional health. It entails a long-term—sometimes, life-long—commitment and dedication to their well-being.

Universal love and compassion goes even further; here, our commitment is eternal, and the scope of our love encompasses all beings, everywhere. It entails a complete and unflinching altruism. The well-being of all-beings is paramount in our consciousness. We apply a higher standard to the words 'happiness' and 'well-being,' for we are not only concerned with immediate and ephemeral needs and pleasures, but with liberation from even the possibility of suffering for everyone. As the Muslim Sufi poet, Hafiz, writes:

> *And love*
> *Says,*
> *"I will, I will take care of you,"*
> *To everything that is*
> *Near.*[46]

The Sufi tradition of Islam encourages a total immersion in love, a universal love that infuses the whole of our being. When we are truly 'in love,' every part of our consciousness, every cell in our body resonates with its sublimity. It is in this divine love that we feel a universal altruism, connectivity, and reciprocity. When we are *in love,* in a sacred way, our constant wish is for the eternal happiness and liberation of all beings everywhere. This is the highest ideal of love. Remember the famous words of Paul in his first letter to the Corinthians:

*Love is patient, love is kind;*
*It does not envy, it does not boast,*
*It is not proud, nor is it rude;*
*It is not self-seeking, nor easily angered,*
*It keeps no record of wrongs.*
*Love does not delight in evil,*
*But rejoices in the truth.*
*Love bears all things, believes all things,*
*Hopes all things, and endures all things.*
*Love never ends.*[47]

This unadulterated being *in love* naturally gives rise to a universal compassion that seeks to free all beings from their suffering. Therefore, Buddhists promise to make compassion their way of being in every second of their lives; they promise to put the well-being of others before themselves; they promise to work to liberate all beings from suffering and the causes of suffering; they promise to work for their happiness.[48]

## REFINING OUR INTENTIONS

All who have really experienced love, know that love is not bounded by the physical body—it is ethereal. It is a cosmic elixir that seeps through the porous shell of our individual consciousness and connects us with others. When this happens, we are together in love. That is to say: in love, we are one. Love is the connective force that can join us all, if we would only release ourselves into its power. Once we are all together in love, there can be no feelings of selfishness, no greed, no anger, no jealously or hatred. From the perspective of true love, why would we want any of those things? Why would we do anything to perpetuate them? When love is remembered and cultivated, discord and division simply vanish.

But we shouldn't wait around, passively expecting to fall in love with everyone, hoping that this will help us to think, feel, and act differently toward them. It is better to actively open to love, to take an attitude of love, and to cultivate it in our lives. For when we look at another person with loving eyes—eyes without judgment, eyes that see things compassionately—it softens and transforms them in our sight. In the reflection of our loving eyes, they trust that they are really loved, they soften toward us, and are awakened to their own inner potential for being in love, both within themselves and with others.

So once we become acquainted with these ways of embracing love and compassion, when we are convinced of their possibilities for our lives, we can learn to be observant of the general state of our ordinary mind when compared with our ideal. When we have a new standard by which to judge our own real intentions, we can begin to raise our aspirations to higher levels

Still, moving ourselves to new levels of intentionality is not easy. This is especially true today, when so much attention is given to 'self-help,' 'self-love,' and 'self-esteem.' We are often blurring the lines between healthy self-improvement and loving ourselves as we really are. Thus, we are sometimes loathe to critique ourselves honestly for fear of lowering our self-esteem or harming our self-image, becoming prey to others who would take advantage of us. We know it is not healthy to feel bad about ourselves, but the consequences of avoiding an honest self-assessment (discussed in Step Three) are far more serious.

If we are really honest with ourselves, we can easily admit that Great Compassion for others is not among our constant intentions. While we may not have malice toward people, generally, and while we may even wish them well for the most part, we do not usually find ourselves 'in love' with strangers and the people we meet on a daily basis. Nor do we think of them with the Great Compassion.

First, there are the difficult people in our lives, people that challenge our ability to be compassionate. Then there are people that we are fairly neutral about; we don't feel one way or another about them. Then there are those whom we like casually, acquaintances or friends of convenience and mutual need. I think it is safe to say that most of our relationships fall into these three categories. Beyond these, are a few people that we really love, and among them a precious few for whom we have unconditional love and compassion. But when we examine our relationships with these few people, can we really say that we are truly compassionate toward them? Are we really committed to and concerned with their eternal happiness? Are we really devoted to seeing the very roots of suffering removed from their lives?

Many years ago, when I first began to observe the actual state of my own compassion, I had to admit that there were very few moments, if any, when I had actually experienced the Great Compassion. Although I might have had the aspiration to be a truly compassionate person, I wasn't one yet. But, having met the Dalai Lama, and a few other extraordinary people, I was confident that it was possible.

Over the years, I continued to experiment with and explore the nuances of altruistic love and Great Compassion. Using Buddhist meditation techniques for generating compassion, I would try to do this with specific people in my life, to see if I could detect a difference in the quality of our relationship. I tried hard to generate unconditional love and Great Compassion for people that I was either neutral about or was having a difficult time with. I would start in meditation then continue practicing while I was interacting with people during the day. Being compassionate when sitting alone in a peaceful atmosphere is one thing, but doing it in the moment is another thing altogether. I wanted to see how it would go when the rubber actually met the road.

I experimented with the idea of being their mother—loving, holding and nurturing them like my own child. When they did something that I found offensive, I tried to trade places with them, seeing the world through their eyes, dealing with the same difficulties they were dealing with. I tried taking on their sadness, their insecurities, giving them my love and desire for healing in return. If someone were sick, I would empathize deeply with them, trying to take on their illness myself, while at the same time, praying for them and feeling healing energy touching and transforming the source of their pain and illness. If one of my employees became bored and ineffective in their job, I would work with them to determine what they were most passionate about and capable of doing, rather than forcing them into a role that didn't fit their capabilities. If someone was angry with me, I tried to feel sympathy for them, in the same way as I might empathize with someone with an open wound. Anger, after all, is just the outward symptom of inner pain, anxiety, frustration, or insecurity.

Through these experiments, I began to distinguish between the different qualities of love. I began to recognize the full spectrum of how I used this word, the variants of its meaning, and I even discovered a kind of hierarchy of values. The purpose of this type of discernment isn't to become judgmental about love, or even of how you love. It is to fine-tune the sense of honesty and humility in the face of what may be the hardest of all virtues, love and compassion.

### DISCERNING TRUE LOVE & COMPASSION

You have probably heard the expression, "You may fool all the people some of the time; you can even fool some of the people all the time; but you can't fool all of the people all the time."[49] This is something to keep in mind, because spiritual practice is not immune to ego-inflation. It is very easy to fool ourselves and others when it comes to the true quality of our spirituality. For our words can make us sound 'spiritual' and 'compassionate,' even when there is little evidence to back it up. It is no wonder that people are often skeptical about those who claim to be 'spiritual.' How many times have they seen charismatic religious figures fall from grace?

Remember, true spirituality is not about charisma; it is not about what you say, it is about what you do, and with what integrity you do it. True love and compassion are determined by the quality of our integrity, by the quality of our lives, and by the demonstration of these qualities in our relationships with others. This is a teaching that is found across the spectrum of spiritual paths, and it is the reason why the karmic consequences of spiritual deceit are more significant than ordinary lies and misrepresentations; for such deceit flies in the very face of this teaching, which is stressed over and over by the founders of the great spiritual traditions.

Many would like to think of spirituality as an environment without judgment, where we agree to say, "I'm okay, you're okay." But if we are truly trying to transform ourselves into loving and compassionate human beings, we must at least learn to say, "You might be okay . . . but I've still got some work to do." Self-honesty, as we noted in Step Three, is critically important to this process, and to spiritual practice in general.

Nevertheless, this discernment around the quality of our love and compassion is not meant to be judgmental, in the sense of seeing oneself as a good or a bad person. It is simply a way to help us develop the kind of love and compassion that can truly help others and ourselves achieve sustainable happiness. So, keeping this in mind, let's look at a few examples of how we love from my own discernment process. Remember, these do represent a template for you to follow, nor are they even especially profound, they are merely examples of the type of process with which you might experiment.

### THE LOVE TRIANGLE OF COMMON INTEREST

Like many of you, I often use the word 'love' in a casual way, saying things like: "I love Indian food," "I love orchids," "I love sailing," or "I love a good glass of wine at the end of a day." Clearly, the word 'love' in these cases refers to an aesthetic or value judgment about the types of things and activities that give us pleasure. Often, we tend to triangulate friendships around the things we love, and love to do together. These shared loves give an enhanced sense of meaning and pleasure to our lives, and sometimes form the basis of our friendships.

It is the same with romantic relationships based on common needs, or common personality characteristics. When we experience these together, we often say, "I love you!" But this type of love is conditional, based upon shared tastes and interests. Once the things we 'love' are unavailable, or circumstances change, many of these relationships simply dissolve. Or when our romantic relationships and sexual appetites begin to wane, we might even say, "I don't love you anymore." So we begin to realize that these so called loves and friendships based on common interests are not reliable vehicles for true and sustainable happiness.

### LOVE BASED ON SHARED PHYSICAL OR PERSONALITY TRAITS

Then there is the person we 'love,' who acts or looks similar to ourselves. This love is predicated upon archetypal matches imprinted in our unconscious mind, or in our sub-conscious when we are very young. We might share certain obvious physical characteristics: we might be of the same race; we might both be tall; perhaps we are both read-haired with blue eyes. We might have a shared body language or way of speaking, be compatible lovers, or have habits that seem to mesh easily. We might both be 'type-A' personalities, or our hopes and dreams might match-up item for item. For all these reasons, we fall madly 'in love' and become totally attached to one another.

But often, relationships based on these unconscious attractions to shared traits are poisoned from the start by projection. We project 'sameness' onto the other, or see them as carriers of our best characteristics. Or we might project the image of our mother or father in them, hoping they will unconditionally love and accept us, perhaps in ways our biological parents didn't. But as we get to know them better, we slowly and painfully begin to realize that they are not the person we *wanted* them to be; they are unique individuals with flaws and foibles, as well as their own best qualities. In short, they are not screens unto which we can simply project what we want. Instead of realizing the truth of this situation, we most often blame them for deceiving us, when it was our own projections that were at fault. Again, we say, "I don't love you anymore."

## LOVE AS A DEBT TO BE REPAID

Once I began aspiring to the Great Compassion, I realized that most of my previous acts of generosity were actually self-serving. I was usually being helpful with the thought of being repaid. So whatever happiness I had in giving was really contingent on a reciprocal repayment. Even then, I wouldn't have been happy with just any repayment, it would have depended on the quality and quantity of the repayment. If I didn't like it or want it, I might have been mad at the person who gave it to me! Therefore, since the repayment is wholly dependent on the other person, our happiness rests in their hands. So there can be no ultimate satisfaction, contentment, or happiness in a gift that requires repayment.

This is obvious enough, but most of us continue in this behavior, even when it doesn't pay-off. We keep on giving selfishly in the hope that, finally, someone will repay us in a way that matches our expectations. If we don't feel fully reciprocated, we feel underappreciated and misused. This is especially true in the case of emotional giving, which is often done with the idea of payback. In this case, we often create 'guilt-chits.' The person to whom we say something nice is made to feel guilty because they haven't given something back to us that we consider of equal value—perhaps even for the compliment we just paid to them! The strategy here, and we all have experienced it, is to say something nice, or give some gift in order to make the recipient feel guilty that they haven't done something equally nice. It is a strategy learned in childhood, and would that it remained there. The creation of guilt is our way of gaining compensation for a favor, compliment, or gift. Guilt makes it impossible for the other person to ever get even with us, so we are always ahead! The result, however, is not happiness, but resentment on both sides.

### Ripening the Seeds of Love & Compassion

Imagine for a moment that our individual consciousness is like a garden. Each of our thoughts, words, and actions are seeds planted in the field of consciousness. The potency of these seeds is determined by the quality of our intention for thinking, speaking, and doing. The quality of the fruit that grows from these seeds is determined by the quality of the intention that accompanied them. The most succulent and delicious fruits are the ones whose plants come from seeds of compassion. The sour ones come from seeds planted with anger, selfishness, and greed.

Meditations on compassion plant seeds deep within our consciousness that ripen according to the intention with which they were planted. Exactly when, where, or how meditative fruit will ripen is determined by our intention for meditating and the other karmic conditions of our life. In our seven-part process, we prepare our garden-like minds through the examination of Motivation, Gratitude, Transformation, and Compassion described in steps One through Four. These can be likened to cultivating a beautiful garden by plowing, fertilizing, weeding, and watering.

These internal laws of cause and effect, modified by our intentions, operate beneath the surface of our normal mental activity; each of our intentional thoughts, words, and actions are like new seeds planted in our consciousness, bearing fruit in the form of consequences, and specifically, in future thoughts and feelings. Generally speaking, 'good intentions' beget thoughts and feelings that support happiness, whereas 'bad intentions' only beget more suffering. Now, love and compassion are the highest forms of intentionality and yield comparable forms of happiness. As our compassion spreads, so does our happiness. The only caveat here is that the thoughts of our own happiness that get mixed-in with our compassionate intentions for others tend to nullify the consequent happiness for us. Therefore, as we begin our meditation on love and compassion, it is very helpful to make sure we are not falling back on some of the common types of self-serving love we mentioned earlier. We must be mindful of our ordinary tendencies and be honest about how we are formulating our highest aspirations.

Based upon my own experiments with love and compassion, I am of the opinion that there will be no world peace or sustainable happiness unless all human beings everywhere embrace love as their religion, and compassion as their credo. In the early part of the 20th-century, the Sufi master, Hazrat Inayat Khan began to call for "a religion of love, harmony, and beauty," saying, "if God is Love, then we, every one of us, can prove God in us by expressing [Love] in our life."[50] This is a realistic intention that we can all get behind, to manifest the sacred in our lives through love. No one else can do this for us, and we cannot expect any sustainable peace or happiness until we wholeheartedly, and unselfishly, begin to dedicate ourselves to the well-being of others. So as we close this section, let us make this silent vow . . .

*"May I Be Loving and Compassionate."*

My love belongs to those
*Who love each other in Me,*
*Who experience intimacy in Me,*
*Who shower each other*
*With goodness for My Sake;*
*And who visit each other*
*Joyfully for My Sake.*

— *Mishkat al-Anwar, Hadith* 88[51]

# STEP FIVE
## MINDFULNESS

## *"May I Be Focused and Mindful Through Breathing"*

Calm, steady, and focused breathing are at the heart of many secular and spiritual techniques of meditation. When we breathe properly, we become less stressed and distracted; we are able to think more clearly, and to focus on the task at hand. Our blood-pressure drops, and our anxiety disappears. Many spiritual traditions teach deep and profound methods of breathing that balance our energies and center our consciousness deep within our being, where we are able to concentrate on our spiritual practice. In this step, we allow our consciousness to recede from our eyes, ears, nose, tongue, touch, thoughts, and emotions. As we breathe gently, our consciousness rides on the subtle breath into our heart center. This is the place that many traditions call 'the seat of the soul,' the core of our consciousness. Residing there, we may begin our own respective meditations, contemplations, and prayers. In this process, we learn to develop the capacity of 'mindfulness,' to achieve tranquil focus, and to dispassionately observe and release our incessant thoughts, emotions, habits, and memories.

# STEP FIVE
## MINDFULNESS

OFTEN, WHEN PEOPLE are first introduced to breathing practice, they think, "Is this it? Just breathing?" It's as if breathing is too mundane to be 'spiritual.' It seems ridiculous that we should focus on something so automatic, something that happens without our notice most of the time. But this is one of the gifts of spiritual practice: to become conscious of all that we usually take for granted; to be present in each moment; to be aware enough to make rational and positive choices; and to end our enslavement to our baser instincts, negative emotions, and cultural conditioning. Thus, we begin with the most basic, the most autonomic process of our bodies—*breathing*. After all, the words 'spirit' and 'breath' are actually synonymous in many languages and traditions.[52]

## A PERSONAL HISTORY OF BREATHING

The truth is, most of the time, we do take breathing for granted; that is, until we are somehow deprived of breath and can't get what we need from it. Only then do we realize how vital and precious this process it really is. For some, this may be something as simple as being extremely winded after running; while for others, it may be as serious as emphysema. For me, it has been a life-long 'relationship' with asthma.

Some of the most vivid memories of my childhood are of struggling to breathe, and feeling the panic that comes with this struggle. For along with the vibrant autumn colors and bountiful crops of Iowa's harvest-time, there is also a mold that comes from the detritus of decaying plants in the rich soil of my homeland. Unfortunately, my asthmatic lungs and sensitive bronchial system had a real problem with this mold. For some unfathomable reason, my autonomic nervous system seemed to want to shut down the air passages to my lungs whenever it encountered this simple airborne life-form, forcing me to struggle for my very life. But struggling only seemed to make the matters worse; so I was often left feeling powerless in the face of this strange internal force. Occasionally, our dear family doctor was even forced to rush over in the middle of the night to give me a shot of adrenalin, just to keep me alive.

My fear of this situation was only heightened as my father recounted the travails of my grandfather who also had asthma, and who had died in his early 60s. I naturally assumed from an early age that this would be my fate as well, and I felt it looming over me with every severe asthma attack. I used to dread those Fall nights, and I prayed for an early frost to kill off the mold so I could breath freely again.

As I got older and seriously pursued my athletic career, I began to find other ways to cope with my asthma. As a high school and college athlete, I learned to watch my breathing closely for the early signs of an impending attack. I would begin my warm-ups more gradually than the other players, thus allowing my metabolism to adjust to the increased activity. If I were able to detect the warning signs early enough, I could focus my mind on the bronchial tubes, visualizing their relaxing and opening, training myself to breath gently and evenly. After doing this for a few minutes, I would usually begin to feel the fresh sensation of air moving unobstructed in and out of my lungs. While this didn't always work, I learned that I wasn't entirely powerless before this condition.

Over the years, I have used a variety of meditation, breathing, and exercise techniques to help control my asthma, and with much success, though I still rely on bronchial inhalers to prevent serious attacks. Although I have not been able to 'cure' my asthma, I have lived beyond my grandfather's 60 years and learned a great deal about breathing and its effects on human physiology and psychology. For instance, I now know that this condition is caused by a combination of physical, psychological, environmental, and even 'karmic' factors, and that meditation techniques can, in many cases, override my autonomic 'circuits' to induce tranquil and fluid breathing. Most importantly, I now see that a contemplative engagement with the deep causes of my asthma can even effect profound healing.

In my case, my mindfulness practice also led to the elimination or reduction of certain foods like wheat (gluten), milk products from cows (lactose), alcohol and refined sugar, all of which seemed to be depleting my energy and causing inflammation in my joints and bronchial tubes. Fortunately, this mindful dietary adjustment eased my asthmatic condition and increased my vitality. So it is clear that we cannot insulate mindfulness from all the other interdependent factors of our lives, like food, exercise, sleep, occupation, kindness and ethical conduct.

For a long time, it simply made no sense to me that my body would rather kill itself than accept this simple organism into my lungs. This, of course, caused me to be intensely curious about the many ways in which certain functions in this organism which we call the body-mind complex over-react to external stimuli. In time, however, and through my own experiments and experiences, I began to make some sense of this. This propensity of our bodies for self-injury seems to reflect the hidden 'injuries' within our unconscious that are calling out to be healed. Thus, when we only address the physical symptom, the symptom persists in subtle and changing ways, as if saying, "Go deeper." But when our healing is actually directed toward the deeper wounds within us, rather than just the physical symptoms, then we are on our way to sustainable health and happiness.

This viewpoint has allowed me to see asthma a valuable teacher in my life, one for which I am deeply grateful. It is has also helped me to experience how meditation can be a profound ally for physical, mental and spiritual well-being.

## BREATHING AS A SPIRITUAL PRACTICE

Breathing is the single most important thing we do every moment of our lives, for air is one of the fundamental constituents of life, carrying the oxygen that nourishes and revitalizes every cell in our body. Through breathing, we inhale oxygen into our lungs, where it is marvelously transferred through the permeable membranes of the alveoli into the red cells in our blood that then transfer it to the trillions of living cells in our body. Most of these cells are not even human, so our breathing supports a vast internal ecosystem of life. Indeed, it is impossible to precisely define the boundaries between 'our own consciousness' and all the human and non-human cells that co-exist in this vastly complex organism we call "our body."

As we breathe in, we inhale the oxygen produced by the plants for our survival. As we breathe out, we exhale the carbon dioxide that plants need for their survival. Mindfully, we breathe ourselves into universal reciprocity with all the physical elements and life-forms on Earth and in the Universe. In this way, breathing itself becomes a deep and profound experience of interdependence and 'inter-being-ness' with all of existence.

The physical health of our brain and neurological system also depend on a constant supply of oxygen. And just as oxygen supports the state of our physical body, the way we breathe effects the psychological state of our mind. For example, breathing in short, quick gasps causes anxiety and fear, while inhaling slowly and deeply promotes calmness and a feeling of security. Therefore, breathing with the intention of calm compassion for all the beings in our inter-dependent inner and outer worlds, promotes the well-being and healing of our mind, body, and spirit.[53]

When breathing, we empty out our lungs in order to receive life-giving oxygen. Each out-breath is an act of faith that another in-breath will follow. It is also the natural process through which we might empty ourselves of the *false self,* which is a prerequisite for being filled up again with the love and wisdom that transcends the limited boundaries of our ordinary states of mind. In doing this, we empty ourselves of our finite, flesh-bound identity in order to be replenished by an infinitely expanded identity that encompasses all of existence.

THE SUBTLE BREATH

But even beyond the obvious importance of oxygen and controlled breathing for our physical and psychological health, there is also a subtler, spiritual aspect to breath. Indeed, many of the world's spiritual systems speak of this refined and subtle dimension of air and breath. For instance, the Indian systems refer to it as *prana,* while the Chinese systems call it qi. This is nothing less than the subtle 'breath of life' that surrounds and permeates all living things. Sometimes it is described in terms of an inextricable connection between the subtlest elemental forms of both consciousness and air; the two 'ride together,' providing the foundation for all sentient life. Although science cannot yet confirm this most subtle connection, accomplished meditation practitioners often observe and experience the workings of this subtle 'energy' in their meditations.

In meditation, therefore, it is very important to pay close attention to the way in which we breathe, and to perceive the subtler and more refined attributes of breath. For example: one tradition instructs us to focus solely on the air as it touches the very tip of our nose, where it touches the skin at the entrance to our nostrils; another instructs us to focus on our belly expanding outward with each breath and contracting inward with each exhalation; still another concentrates on feeling the breath as it pervades every nook and cranny of the body, from the top of head to tips of the toes and fingers; and yet another teaches us to visualize our inhalations as expanding even beyond the boundaries of our skin.

Then there are the esoteric traditions that tell us how to move this subtle breath, the life-force called *prana* or *qi,* through the nadis (subtle vessels) and chakras (plexuses) that make up our spiritual anatomy. One method for doing this uses a technique called *pranayama,* which teaches us to open and close our right and left nostrils in alternating cycles, moving the *prana* through the right and left 'channels,' and causing it rise through the central channel, opening the chakras and actualizing our full spiritual potential.[54]

What all these types of breathing have in common is the capacity for undistracted focus and unwavering introspection. Conscious, intentional breathing helps to alleviate the distraction of random sensations, emotions, and thoughts, as well as to develop a profound practice of spiritual depth. So, to center and interiorize our minds, we simply focus on our breathing. In this way, we open ourselves to universal love, healing, and wisdom; our consciousness begins to follow our breath through the channels of our body into our heart center, in which we realize the most profound truths of our existence and are liberated from suffering.

## My Early Training

As I mentioned earlier, I was introduced to Buddhism by His Holiness, the Dalai Lama in 1970, and soon after, was sent by him to Geshe Rabten to receive my first instruction in Buddhist meditation. His Holiness told me that Geshe Rabten was a great scholar and meditator who was at that time in the middle of a long meditation retreat in the mountains, a few miles above the Dalai Lama's residence.

Since I hadn't yet learned Tibetan, Tenzin Geshe, the Dalai

Lama's private secretary introduced me to a brilliant young Tibetan reincarnate Lama named Gonsar Tulku. Gonsar's English was excellent, and he was kind enough to translate for me when I went to see Geshe Rabten (whom I addressed as 'Geshe-la')[55] every other day for a month. I will always remember our talks as we walked up dirt paths through trees and fields with the snow-capped foothills of the Himalayas as a backdrop. After about an hour of steady walking, we would see the small, one-room hut of my new teacher near a clump of trees across a broad meadow. The walls were constructed of mud which had been white-washed, and the roof was made of wooden timbers and tiles. As we approached, a Tibetan monk would spot us coming and walk out to greet us. This was Geshe-la's cook and 'lookout.' He was there each day to make sure that no one unexpectedly disturbed the silence of Geshe-la's solitary retreat.

On our first visit, the cook greeted Gonsar warmly, for he was an important student of Geshe-la, and welcomed me as well. But he asked us to wait a bit until the time was right to enter the hut where Geshe-la had remained in meditation for many months. I felt a nervous anticipation growing inside me as I waited. I was worried that my questions would not be worthy of his attention, and that my intention was not pure enough to deserve disturbing the silence of this great teacher.

After a short wait, we entered the little hut where Geshe-la sat alone on a mat and cushion on a smooth, clean dirt floor. Gonsar bowed three times on the floor as I stood just outside the door, peering into the dark room. When the prostrations had finished, Gonsar introduced me as the one the Dalai Lama had recommended for teaching. I presented Geshe-la with several varieties of fruit I had carried there as an offering and I was invited to sit down on the floor in front of him.

Geshe-la's face bore a friendly, yet, no-nonsense expression. His eyes were deep and relaxed, and his cross-legged body barely moved from a position I imagined he had maintained for hours, days, weeks, and months. He asked me a bit about myself, why I was in India, and how I found myself in the hills above Dharamsala. Then, he asked me why I wanted to study Buddhism.

"To understand the nature of mind," I said.

"In order to understand the nature of mind," he replied, "you must learn to meditate."

With that, he began to teach me how to meditate. He explained how important it was to make the mind one-pointed and tranquil. Once my mind was trained, it could be used to achieve profound realizations about the nature of mind and all that exists. He taught me how to cross my legs and sit with an erect, yet relaxed spine; how to hold my hands right over left in my lap with the tips of my thumbs gently touching each other; how to keep my eyes just slightly open and the tip of my tongue slightly touching the roof of my closed mouth. He described how to begin by smoothly breathing in and out, and how to follow my breath. Then he described how to begin to hold an object like a sacred syllable or image of the Buddha steadily in my mind.

In later sessions, he would describe the nine stages of this meditation, called *shi ney* in Tibetan and *shamatha* in Sanskrit, and how to counteract the obstacles of meditation, like drowsiness, aches and pains, distraction, excitement, and dullness. He told me how I could expect to gradually develop my meditative skills until my mind would become one-pointed, tranquil, and ready for the next stages of meditative practice when I could work with Tantric systems of spiritual transformation.[56]

He said it was very important to develop the capacity to watch my mind while meditating. It was critically important that I learn to observe my thoughts objectively. For, like a thief, these thoughts sneak-in unnoticed and steal away my attention, distracting me from the main purpose of my meditation. He said that this type of mindfulness would be important in all aspects of my life, and in all types of meditation I would pursue in the future. He called this mental capacity, "the mental spy." It sits quietly, hidden away from the rest of the mind's activities, and observes what is going on. Often, he said, when a thought sneaks into the mind and is seen by our internal spy, the uninvited guest becomes embarrassed and simply runs away, disappearing from of the mind.

My first month of training was very difficult for me. I found it nearly impossible to sit still and quiet my mind, and I wasn't sure I was up to the task. As I sat alone in my room after a meeting with Geshe-la, or on the promontory overlooking the vast plains of India, I realized that meditation was the hardest thing I had ever tried to do.[57] It now seemed that the rigorous athletic training and academic study I had done in the years previously were easy compared to simply sitting quietly and trying to focus my mind in one-pointed attention on an object.

## MINDFULNESS – OUR INTERNAL ALLY

One of the most important lessons that I took away from my teacher in that solitary meditation hut high above Dharamsala, apart from the discipline of meditation, was his teaching about "the mental spy." For, in addition to showing me how to adjust my posture, to follow my breath, and concentrate, he also taught me how to observe the inner workings of my mind. Once the mental spy is engaged, it simply begins to operate quietly in the background. This aspect of our consciousness observes the other parts, and keeps us aware of the 'background noise,' as well as the constant fluctuations of our mind. As our capacity to observe becomes more and more refined, we can even see the most subtle interactions between sensations, emotions, conceptualizations, words, and actions. We realize how our words and interactions with others are being controlled by the unconscious, inner workings of our minds. Since these activities of the mind often take place 'under the radar' of our conscious minds, we call them the inner forces of our unconscious mind. When we shine the light of awareness on all of this 'background noise,' it often subsides without further effort on our part. Gradually, our mental spy refines its capacities for observation until nothing escapes its grasp. As Geshe Rabten said to me, "Once discovered by our mental spy, the intruder vanishes into the night, like a burglar who has been caught in the act."

Through years of meditation, I leaned to observe how the mind is constantly 'multi-tasking' beneath our conscious awareness. Simultaneously, the river of our mind carries currents of thought, memory, emotion, sensation, habit, addiction, perception, and concept, all at the same time. Our state-of-mind is totally controlled by these unseen currents. I learned that we can modulate and control these currents by cultivating other states of mind that, when trained, can also operate beneath the surface, channeling our consciousness in positive directions. These internal allies include remembering, concentrating, observing, persevering, focusing, patience and quiescence. When these allies are at work, we can harnesses the vast potential of our minds for happiness, tranquility, compassion, wisdom, and service to others.

ATTRIBUTES OF MINDFULNESS

The term 'mindfulness' is widely used to describe a whole genre of meditational practices derived from the ancient practices of Theravada Buddhism. But like the Americanization of Yoga, some popular mindfulness meditations tend to eschew their spiritual roots in Buddhism, rarely advancing beyond the preliminary steps found in the ancient teachings, focusing on short-term physical and psychological benefits instead.[58] Nevertheless, in my experience, mindfulness is actually a general term for a broad category of helpful mental attributes that are especially important for cultivating a sustainable and satisfying practice of meditation. Once cultivated, they prove their value in all aspects of one's life. The following are the five attributes of mindfulness that have been most helpful to me:

## 1. Remembering

First is the attribute of remembering the object to be meditated on. Here, our object of meditation will depend on our spiritual tradition and spiritual purpose. Different objects might include our breath, a sacred syllable, a *mantra,* a prayer, or an image of a divine being. In order to maintain focus, we must cultivate the attribute of 'remembering.' This is a skill that is sharpened by effort and repetition.

## 2. Concentration and Attention

Second is concentration, the attribute of our consciousness that enables us to sustain focus on the object. Meditative concentration becomes a lot easier once we have a steady and consistent motivation (Step One of InterSpiritual Meditation), a transformative goal (Step Three), and the compassionate intention to help others (Step Four). In other words, we need to be firmly convinced of the need to concentrate to prevent our minds from wandering.

## 3. Observation or Vigilance

Third is the attribute of observation, sometimes referred to as the 'mental spy.' This function of our consciousness sits quietly in the shadows of our awareness, alerting us to any intruders. It bears witness to our inner mental events

us to stop negative thoughts and emotions from
into hurtful words and actions. Once fully trained
ated, our internal witness is capable of spotting
memories, and emotions, even before they even
into our minds. Observation enables our minds to
maintain meditative focus.

## 4. Re-focusing

Fourth is the capacity to return to the object of meditation
after a moment of distraction. As we cultivate the capacity
of inner observation, we experience fewer moments of
distraction. With each distraction, however, we need to
return immediately. Therefore, our capacity for re-focusing
on the object must be cultivated and refined. We do this
through patient perseverance in meditative practice over
many months and years.

## 5. Patience

Fifth is the attribute of patience, an absolutely essential
component of mindfulness practice. Our minds are in
constant motion. Like the ocean, we generally only see the
currents and waves on the surface. But, like the ocean, there
are the deep currents and cross currents that are always
at work in the depths that influence each moment of our
conscious awareness, our emotions, our choices, our words
and our actions. As we deepen our meditation, we become
aware of these subtle undercurrents and how they can
disturb our quietude and focus. When we become aware and
distracted by these, we tend to loose our tranquil focus. If
we become anxious, upset and try too hard, the distractions
will multiply. Therefore, we need to be patient with ourselves
so we don't become discouraged and give up. When we are
patient, we can gently persevere, refocus on our breath and
return to quietude. We become free from the unsettling
undercurrents that generally dictate our state of mind and
the rhythm of our lives. It is a subtle and delicate dance.
Patience helps us to gently guide and control our minds as
preparation for the next step in our meditation.

## 6. Quiescence

Sixth is the attribute of mental quiescence and tranquility that arises from meditative absorption. Although quiescence is a natural capacity of our mind, it generally takes time, patience, and perseverance to cultivate. Mature meditators, however, learn not to lose focus or become distracted by tranquility when it morphs into a more exhilarating and blissful states that draw us away from our central meditative purpose. Our witnessing consciousness, or mental spy, must also inform us of any impending narcissistic pleasures that may lead us away from our compassionate intentions. While subtle and refined quiescence can accompany us throughout our waking and dreaming, extreme bliss can lead us toward more selfish ends, possibly crashing into states of emotional instability and suffering. So, as with any other mental state, we simply observe the bliss and return to the evenness of quiescence and tranquil focus.

By cultivating our breathing and mindfulness, we gain life-long partners that can help us to be successful in all aspects of our lives. Once we have invested in this practice, we will find that it pays major dividends in daily life, improving our mental acuity, making us more efficient in our work, and improving our relationships with others. It also helps us to become acutely aware of the psychological, conceptual, and emotional causes of stress which, in turn, are the cause of many health problems.

By now it should be clear that the long-term by-products of meditative breathing and mindfulness, which are causes of good health and happiness, far outweigh the temporary peace of mind we feel in meditation practice. From my own experience, and from conversations with other experienced meditators, I have learned that each of us must embark on a life-long experiment in breathing and mindfulness in order to discover the true benefits of meditation. We must accept personal responsibility for developing our own practice, and commit to it as a true path of self-discovery and transformation. At the same time, it is very important to find reliable, authentic teachers that can critique our practice and offer sound advice on ways to refine it; for each contemplative tradition will have its own terms and methods for cultivating the attributes of mindfulness.

CENTERING THROUGH THE BREATH

In many traditions, meditation begins with and arises from a process of centering or interiorizing our awareness. We cannot enter into tranquil, undistracted meditation as long as our consciousness is continually distracted by sensory input from the eyes, ears, nose, tongue, and our sense of touch. Thus, we must withdraw the dominant part of our awareness from the senses and habitual patterns which receive most of our attention on a daily basis. Ordinarily, the only time we are not attached to external sense objects is when we are asleep, or when we are concentrating deeply on something. The sensory detachment of meditation, however, is different than sleep in that we are conscious and alert during meditation. It is similar to deep concentration in that our mind stays fixed, or rather continues to bring its attention back to its object, the breath, a sound, a syllable, an image, a concept, an area of the body, or to a divine principle or being.

It is very important to develop a method for withdrawing our awareness from the senses if we are going to meditate effectively. Many traditions teach us to bring our consciousness into the heart, which is often described as the 'seat of the soul,' the abode of our core consciousness, or the center of our being.[59] This placement of the 'soul' or 'core consciousness' within the territory of the heart in the body is described in both the exoteric and esoteric traditions of Hinduism, Buddhism, Taoism, Judaism, Christianity, and Islam. In the exoteric traditions, the references are usually very general and metaphorical, while in the esoteric traditions, a subtle 'spiritual anatomy' underlying our physical form is often described in great detail. This feature of our spiritual anatomy is often regarded as the subtle template for the physical body.

Once we have withdrawn our sensory awareness into the subtle consciousness of the heart-center, we can enter into the pristine clarity of direct wisdom. The nature of this wisdom is often likened to a pure 'white' or 'clear light,' and is described in Buddhism as the unstained consciousness that emerges at the time of death, suddenly unfettered by the limitations of the five senses and the ignorance, or limited mental awareness of human existence.[60] When accessed and activated, this wisdom-awareness has the power to perceive the truth of existence directly, to eliminate the obstacles to enlightenment, and to purify our eternal consciousness.

Although similar notions are found in a number of traditions, I want to stress that there are significant differences between the names and descriptions ascribed to this process, and perhaps even in the ultimate experience attained by adepts of each tradition. Therefore, it should be remembered that I am only speaking from my own perspective; you must feel free to find your way through this territory, and to utilize the teachings that come from a tradition that is comfortable for you.

Now, while it is not necessary to make these views of the different spiritual traditions a part of your meditation practice, it is important to have a sense of the general context in which mindfulness is cultivated, and the layered depths to which some traditions take this process of centering. So we needn't believe in these more esoteric teachings in order for this method of centering to have beneficial effects on our mind and body. In some ways, it is better to have a very simple focus. This is why most practitioners (even very mature ones) use the breath as the foundation of their practice; for it is perhaps the most vital process of the body that we can focus on with relative ease.

Therefore, both spiritual and non-spiritual meditation practices tend to focus on breathing, and whether or not we believe in the various interpretations of 'soul,' 'core consciousness,' or the 'spirit-body,' it is still useful for us to detach our awareness from the external senses and to gradually withdraw to that area of the chest that is the center of our breathing. With or without the spiritual overlay on this process, physical centering through breathing is extremely important for maintaining a calm, compassionate mind, and a relaxed, healthy body.

## AN IMAGINAL BREATHING PRACTICE

The following description should be treated as general guidance for gradually deepening one's own process of centering. In an InterSpiritual group meditation, each person should use the techniques that are taught in their tradition, or by their own teacher. If you don't have a technique, or wish to try something new, you might try the following technique:

Either sit cross-legged on a cushion, or on a chair with your back straight (but not rigid) with your feet flat on the floor. Place your hands comfortably on your lap, assuming the hand-position that is appropriate to your tradition. If you don't have a specific hand-position, simply place the palms of your hands down on the tops of your thighs, roughly equidistant between your hip-joint and knees. Feel relaxed within your body and fully present in this place.

Gently close your eyes until there is just a sliver of light coming in. Place the tip of your tongue on the roof of your mouth just behind your upper front teeth and keep your lips together very gently. Then begin inhaling and exhaling softly and evenly through your nose, and simply relax into the silence.

As you breathe in, imagine that you are inhaling the healing energy of the universe. To help with your visualization, imagine the air has a color, perhaps a light iridescent blue. Feel the pure healing of this iridescent blue air entering the very edge of your nostrils, going up through your nasal passages, down the back of your throat, into your bronchial tubes, and filling your lungs.

As you continue to breathe in, you can visualize this delicately colored iridescent air gradually spreading throughout your entire body, extending out to the ends of your toes and fingers.

Now, exhale slowly and imagine that you are releasing all the toxins and diseases from within your body, all of the aches and pains dissipating with the exhalation.

Now, inhale the calm and peaceful energy of the universe; feel it penetrating every cell in your body.

Then, exhale all of the stress, anger and anxiety that may have been polluting your mind and body.

Continue this breathing for a few minutes until you feel relaxed and find your attention leaving the external world and turning inward. Then allow your conscious awareness to follow your breath from the tip of your nose, through your sinus cavities, down the back of your throat, through your bronchial tubes, and into your lungs. Feel your chest cavity as it rises and falls, and even the beat of your heart as it pumps oxygen throughout your body.

At the end of each inward breath, hesitate for a few moment to give your conscious awareness a chance to rest and reside there. Then exhale evenly and slowly until your lungs are empty.

Before breathing in, hesitate for a few moments, leaving a little space between the exhalation and the next inhalation. Then, breathing in again, draw your consciousness into your heart area. As you do this over time, your ability to withdraw your consciousness into your 'heart center' will gradually increase, and you will learn to rest in the center of your being.

Now, slowly begin to cultivate the capacity for inner observation and vigilance, allowing the witnessing function of your consciousness to observe all the other mental events as they rise and fall. Your internal witness will make you aware of all the other things that are going on inside your mind. As you see thoughts, emotions, memories, or bodily aches arise, just notice them and let them go, like white clouds dissolving in a clear blue sky.

Gently return to your breathing and feel the natural state of relaxation and tranquility that emerges from one-pointed focus on the breath.

This form of breathing is actually sufficient by itself for some types of mediation. It creates deep relaxation and a calm clarity; it clears the mind and it helps the body to heal.[61] In fact, an entire meditation session could be devoted solely to this particular breathing practice, or other such breathing practices. In this fifth stage of InterSpiritual Meditation, you may employ the centering and breathing techniques that are most appropriate for you, or those that are recommended in your own tradition. If you do not know what technique should be used, or have not been instructed in one, you may choose to try one of the basic techniques given Part Three of this book.

For some, the breathing process begun in Step Five will continue to be the primary focus of Step Six, and for others it will only serve as a preliminary step. This is because mindful breathing meditation is often foundational for a more extensive meditation practice. Therefore, mindful breathing may be practiced as a 'way into' another meditation, or it may be used as a sovereign practice which may be taken deeper and deeper. So as we close this section, let us make this silent vow . . .

*"May I Become Focused and Mindful Through Breathing."*

*Empty yourself of everything.*
*Let the mind become still.*
*The ten thousand things rise and fall*
*While the Self watches their return.*
*They grow and flourish*
*And then return to the source.*
*Returning to the source is stillness,*
*Which is the way of nature.*

— Lao Tzu, *Tao Te Ching*, 16[62]

# STEP SIX

## MEDITATION

### *"May I Become Wise Through Meditation"*

*Now that the garden of our mind has been carefully cultivated, we can begin to deepen and expand the scope of our meditation. Honoring the profound and marvelous diversity among the world's contemplative traditions, we silently engage in the meditation of our own tradition or choosing, opening to transcendent insight, deep tranquility, or unity with that which is sacred to us. Mindful breathing itself can remain our sole focus or may provide a foundation for our chosen meditation.*

# STEP SIX
## MEDITATION

MY INITIAL TRAINING with Geshe Rabten and extensive study with Geshe Sopa were just the beginning of my journey with meditation. In the forty years since then, my attempts to sustain and deepen my practice have been both challenging and rewarding. Challenging, because it has often been hard to maintain a daily practice; there have been some days when the benefits of meditating were not at all apparent to me. However, there have also been many days when meditation has led to deep tranquility and compassion, and has opened the way for experiences and insights that had eluded my ordinary states of mind.

Generally, it isn't a good idea to try to describe the effects and experiences of one's personal meditation practice. Our words are often inaccurate, as they sometimes diminish or overstate the experience. Our performance-based ego can cause inflation or false modesty. The inherent subjectivity of meditation experiences can also elicit in others the extremes of skepticism or envy.

While modern neuroscience is pin-pointing how meditation 'lights up' various places in the brain that that correspond to happiness and well-being, science is not able to quantify the quality of the wisdom, the bliss, or the love that then ensues. In my experience, the evidence lies in the kindness, compassion and wisdom exhibited by the meditator. 'The proof,' as they say, 'is in the pudding.'

As I observed my own process through the years, and that of some of my peers, I witnessed how we often mistook 'way-points' on our spiritual journey for profound accomplishments.[63] Many began as spiritual warriors only to discover the wisdom of surrender. We often fell into the trap of pride; for it was easy build a false sense of self-importance around being practitioners of Buddhist, Sufi, Indigenous, or Hindu traditions. In my case, I saw how my fellow converts to Tibetan Buddhism often took false pride in their knowledge of Tibetan and Sanskrit languages, their experiences with the Dalai Lama, or their life in Buddhist monasteries. But I have since learned that there is no pride more pathetic than the arrogance of a spiritual practitioner whose identity is built around such associations. One can only do the work, and be satisfied with having done it today. Thus, my personal experience with meditation and spirituality has brought me face-to-face with both the profound and profane aspects of spiritual practice and to notice this same condition among practitioners of other traditions.

For this reason, I have learned to seek out good teachers and methods of meditation that could build on and expand my personal experience, that could challenge and help me to remove the blinders of my own biases, habits, and conditioning. I have also learned that the quality and power of my meditation is inextricably linked to the overall intentions and actions of my day-to-day life. But perhaps the most important thing I have learned is to take responsibility for my own meditation process.[64]

I have also learned that it is nearly impossible to enter immediately into a deep state of meditation without gradually preparing and cultivating our mind as we would a garden. That is why there are five steps gradually leading up to this step. Now, we engage in a specific meditation practice that we have carefully chosen from a tradition that is compatible with our beliefs, reason, temperament and spiritual style. For example, it might be Christian Centering Prayer, or Sufi zikr, or a Hindu mantra practice, or a Native American chant, or the Prayer of the Heart, or a Buddhist focus of Emptiness. Once our mind is properly prepared, then we might also be better prepared to enter into the depth of the meditation that is appropriate for us.

Therefore, this chapter, though called "Meditation," is not meant to tell you what you should be meditating on, or exactly how to take your meditation deeper. It is simply the step or stage in the InterSpiritual Meditation process in which one enters into the deep meditation practice of one's own choosing. Obviously, in a group setting, the practice you are doing may not be the same as that of the person next to you. Nevertheless, you will still be sharing similar intentions and the same InterSpiritual process. If you are in a group, there may be occasions when one member wishes to lead everyone in the same meditation practice at this stage, but you must always be ready to do your own personal work.

So how does Step Six on Meditation differ from Step Five on Mindfulness? The difference lies in the fact that the stable breathing practice begun in Step Five is meant to be preliminary to and a preparation for the meditation done in Step Six. Of course, you may continue with the breathing and mindfulness practice begun in Step Five, taking it to new levels of depth in Step Six, but you may also choose to do another type of meditation practice entirely. For, once again, breathing meditation is a foundational practice, establishing a stable and tranquil basis for other meditation practices as well. Therefore, either option may be pursued in Step Six.

## SOME VARIETIES OF MEDITATION

As I have said before, meditation speaks to the capacity of human consciousness to become disciplined, focused, tranquil, and one-pointed, compassionate and wise. It can guide and calm us in times of stress, sickness, pain and death. Thus, it has sometimes been likened to a sturdy boat that transports our consciousness through the rough seas of life to the other shore of enlightenment and happiness. Nevertheless, there are also subtle aspects of meditation practice that cannot be so neatly categorized or summarized. So it is perhaps worth taking a little time to discuss the functions of meditation, and to talk a little more about the difference between meditation and contemplation.

### Two Functions of Meditation

One way to distinguish between the myriad types of meditation is by *function*. And here I will draw on classical Buddhist definitions, as these might help us to recognize similar approaches in other traditions.

The first category of meditation in Buddhism is called *shamatha,* 'calm abiding,' which emphasizes the function of mental stability, tranquility, one-pointed focus, and mindfulness. The second category is called *vipashyana,* or 'insight,' emphasizing the function of insight, analysis, and wisdom.[65] In this context, Step Five is a *shamatha*-type meditation and Step Six is a *vipashyana*-type meditation.

The meditations that fall into the first category seek to bring the mind to a one-pointed, tranquil focus in which there is no distraction, often employing breathing, visualization, movement, or chanting techniques. The primary purpose of these *shamatha*-type meditations is to be totally focused and absorbed on a meditative 'object.' Such objects include the breath, mantric syllables, and iconographic images. Focused and absorbed attention on these objects often leads to a transcendent experience of peace, tranquility, quiescence, and for some, a non-dual experience of the Divine. Other practices, like devotional prayer, sacred dance, prostrations, and chanting may also partake of this single-pointed focus and absorption, and likewise lead to similar ends.

*Vipashyana*-type meditations both include and build on the *shamatha*-type meditations, supplementing them with other processes for generating a specific wisdom or insight about the 'true nature' of the object of meditation. In Christianity, this wisdom might be of the Trinity dwelling within us and manifesting as a unity with God, as experienced through the process of meditation.[66] In Buddhism, it might include the central and interrelated concepts of Impermanence, Compassion and Emptiness. In Hinduism, it might involve the realization that the limited self-image *(jiva)* is not the true Self *(atman),* and that the true Self is identical with the Ultimate Reality *(Brahman).*

In these 'insight' types of meditation, the meditator is also able to hold the mind in a single-pointed, tranquil focus on a specific object, and then to analyze or discern its nature, or the factors that have brought it into being. With practice, what might begin on a very conceptual (analytical) level may, in time, transition to a non-conceptual, intuitive level, whereby one can discern the truth of something without thinking discursively about it. This direct, unmediated (perhaps even, non-dual) perception of the Ultimate Reality is the goal of many meditative traditions (although the nature and name of this reality may vary between traditions). Particularly strong examples of this latter type of meditation may be seen in the Gelugpa tradition of Tibetan Buddhism and the Habad Hasidic tradition of Judaism, which emphasize rigorous learning and intense contemplative exercises based on reasoning. The meditations of these traditions are especially good for those types of practitioners who crave a strong intellectual underpinning for their practice.

## DISTINGUISHING BETWEEN
## MEDITATION AND CONTEMPLATION

At this point, it is important to remind ourselves of the two broad categories discussed earlier: meditation and contemplation. As we said before, these terms have both been used in different traditions to designate a state of mind that is not influenced by random sensory stimuli, or distracted by extraneous thoughts or emotions. However, in modern parlance, contemplation is generally associated with thinking about, or considering something deeply. In the spiritual context, this might be a contemplation of a sacred reading, an oral teaching, or a spiritual concept. Meditation, on the other hand, has more and more come to be associated with specific techniques for calming and focusing the mind to achieve a specific mental, physical, or spiritual state of being.

In my own experience, spiritual contemplation is a state of consciousness that lies at the borderline between deep thinking and one-pointed meditation. It is deeply concentrated in the service of profound inner observation, insight, analysis, and intuition. Contemplation can both involve and surpass the intellect. It can arise, for example, while sitting in silence, reading, being in nature, engaging in music or art. Contemplation is our means to consciously traverse the borderlands between the sacred and the profane, ecstasy and agony, tragedy and comedy, the mystical and the conceptual, duality and non-duality, the divisive and the unitive. Therefore, subtle and refined contemplative states of mind are often best expressed through such art forms as poetry, painting or calligraphy, music and dance, and even gardening.

In Buddhism, contemplation and meditation go hand in hand. Classical Buddhist education proceeds through three distinct stages: learning, contemplating, and meditating. Generally, meditation is preceded by periods of learning and deep contemplation. Yet meditation can also provide the ground for further contemplation. Indeed, the first four steps of our seven-part process are forms of contemplation. They help us to prepare the mind for a single-pointed meditation and provide context and an aesthetic for a sustainable spiritual practice. Following meditation, we might also reflect deeply, contemplating the experiences of the meditation itself and the techniques we used to catalyze a specific experience. For example, we might observe that a certain breathing technique or body posture was particularly helpful, or we might reflect on a difficult period of distraction, its causes and antidotes. Therefore, contemplation is an important ally of meditation.

These two attributes of our consciousness—meditation and contemplation—support each other in the process of spiritual maturation. However, it is important to be mindful and observant about which function we want to be our primary focus during a given period of meditative activity. Generally, it isn't a good idea to slip back and forth between them in an undisciplined manner, for meditation is a specific form of mind training that requires discipline. Likewise, we need to make sure that we are not using the idea of contemplation simply as a justification for our mental 'wanderings.' Choose a particular focus for your session and try to stay close to it throughout.

A SAMPLE MEDITATION PRACTICE

The following meditation is a simple extension of the practice given in Step Five. Although it is merely an example, you might find it useful as a way into your own meditation.

*Resting in the Heart Center — Shamatha*

We enter this meditation with a calm and relaxed focus on our breathing, and with the vigilant observer operating in the background.

Let your awareness follow the flow of air as it enters your nose. Allow your consciousness to ride on the subtle energy of this refined breath as it nourishes and enlivens all the cells of your body.

Pay attention to the air as it passes through your nasal cavities, gently moving down the back of your throat, past your larynx and into the top of your lungs, filling and expanding them.

As the air penetrates deeply into your lungs, your awareness follows it, becoming conscious of the stream of air connecting and passing from the end of your nose, deep into your breath-center at the bottom of your lungs, deep in the belly, pervading the whole of your being, even expanding beyond your body into the space around you.

Turn on the internal light of vigilant observation, allowing it to passively watch for the arising of any extraneous thoughts, emotions, desires, or memories. As you notice these, simply release them, allowing them to float over the horizon of your sky-like mind. If there are noises or movements in the space around you, treat them as opportunities for passive observation and return to the breath.

As you repeat this process with each inhalation and exhalation, your consciousness gradually begins to depart from the sense organs, becoming concentrated in the heart-center.

Let it remain there, delicately cradled in the center of your chest as you continue this subtle breathing.

## Cultivating Insight and Wisdom — Vipashyana

With your consciousness resting in the center of your chest, feel the beating of your heart as it pounds and reverberates within you.

Now silently imagine and give rise to a prayer, a sacred word or syllable vibrating within and arising from your stomach, finally resounding within the subtle center of your being. This sound connects you with the truth or essence of your existence.

As you say this prayer, word, or syllable with sacred intent, feel it vibrating and saying itself from the depths of your being, allowing your consciousness to be fully focused on it.

This is a delicate process, for you are emptying, releasing and allowing your finite consciousness to give way and dissolve into the core of eternal consciousness and the very essence of your being.

This will take patience; it is a delicate dance that cannot be forced or hurried. Simply relax into this state-of-being and allow it to happen. Empty your limited notions of self and the absolute. Gradually, your self-emptying, along with your prayer, word, or sacred syllable will start to say itself as you are gently absorbed in the divine mystery that lies within and beyond you.

\* \* \* \*

The underlying assumption of many spiritual traditions is that the process of meditation is able to uncover, reveal and release the unbounded inner wisdom that is the intrinsic capacity of every living being. It is through this wisdom that we are able to fulfill our intention to serve the highest interests of all our fellow beings through unbounded love and compassion.

The extreme subtlety and gentleness of this process is described in mystical poetry as the coming together of two lovers in the sacred embrace of non-dual union. The depth of this experience is often compared with sexual intercourse, because its extreme pleasure bears a faint resemblance to ecstasy from merging the self with the sacred, even though the physical act pales in comparison to the unspeakable bliss of sacred union.

This experience is preceded by a combination of pure intention, spiritual maturity, and meditative acumen. Words can only provide rough approximations for this experience. Attempting to name the nameless and to quantify the unquantifiable will only push it further beyond our reach. For it cannot be found only through the intellect or senses, it cannot be physically embraced only by the body, nor named only by the conceptual mind. The unity of our pure consciousness with the sacred cannot be boxed and limited, forced or chased; it can only be joined through the purity of our intention in the sanctity of our own mystic heart.

So as we close this section, let us make this silent vow . . .

*"May I Become Wise Through Meditation."*


*"Instruct me, Sir."*
*Thus Narada approached Sanatkumara. [. . .]*

*"Contemplation, verily, is greater than thought.*
*For the earth, as it were, contemplates;*
*The atmosphere, as it were, contemplates;*
*Heaven, as it were, contemplates;*
*Water, as it were, contemplates;*
*The mountains, as it were, contemplate;*
*Gods and human beings, as it were, contemplate.*
*Therefore the one who attains greatness has,*

*So to say, a share in contemplation.*
*Small-minded people are*
*Quarrelsome, wicked, and slanderous,*
*Whereas the excellent have, so to say,*
*A share in contemplation.*
*Meditate on contemplation.*

*"One who meditates*
*On contemplation as Brahman,*
*Their freedom will extend to*
*The limits of the realm of contemplation,*
*One who meditates on contemplation as Brahman."*

*"But, sir, is there anything greater than contemplation?"*

*"Yes, there is something greater than contemplation."*

*"Then please, sir, tell me about it!"*

*"Wisdom, verily, is greater than contemplation.*
*For by wisdom one knows heaven and earth,*
*Air and atmosphere, water and fire,*
*Gods, human beings, and animals, grass and trees,*
*Right and wrong, true and false, pleasant and unpleasant,*
*Food and drink, this world and the other . . .*
*All these are known by wisdom.*
*Meditate on wisdom.*

*"One who meditates on wisdom as Brahman,*
*Attains the worlds of wisdom and of knowledge.*
*Their freedom will extend to the limits of the realm of wisdom,*
*One who meditates on wisdom as Brahman."*

*— Chandogya Upanishad, VII, 6:1-7:2*[67]

# STEP SEVEN

## DEDICATION

## "May I Serve All Beings with Compassion, Peace, and Wisdom"

*In order for our meditation to have a positive and sustainable impact on our lives, and to truly benefit others, we conclude our meditation by rededicating ourselves to serving the highest good for everyone. As we visualize our family, friends, enemies, colleagues, communities and beings throughout the world, we vow to help alleviate their suffering and bring love, peace and happiness to all. May this meditation help us to engage in the world with wisdom and compassion.*

# STEP SEVEN
## DEDICATION

As I MENTIONED EARLIER, in the mid 1970s, I was fortunate to receive a Fulbright Fellowship to study and complete my Ph.D. dissertation, and to begin researching a series of films I would later make in India.[68] The fellowship stipulated that I be based in Varanasi (Benares), the holy city situated on the banks of the Ganges River. While I was grateful and honored to receive this award, I dreaded the thought of living in Varanasi. My hope was to live and study with my Tibetan teachers in their respective monasteries and to deepen my experience of monastic living. And I was able to do just that the following year, but for the first year at least, I was obligated to live in Varanasi, a city revered by Hindus throughout the world. Even now, I am little embarrassed by my negative knee-jerk response to this great opportunity.

I had visited Varanasi a number of times, and had even lived for many months in the lovely village of Sarnath, about 25 miles away.[69] The sacred aspects of Varanasi fascinated me, but its more profane aspects repelled me. There were myriad temples, holy men and women, pilgrims, and burning *ghats* (where bodies were cremated), surrounded by a cacophony of shops and vendors, shouts and loud-speakers amplifying the chants of Hindu priests. The streets were jammed with all manner of creatures and contraptions—cows, water buffalo, camels, elephants, dogs, bicyclists, pedestrians, cars, auto-rickshaws, and enormous trucks. The city was a teaming tapestry of wonderful and discomforting sights, smells, and sounds. It may be holy, but it is not exactly peaceful. And while, for some, the prospect of living there might have seemed a dream come true, I just couldn't imagine myself being happy in Varanasi.

Nevertheless, I settled into a relatively quiet part of the town where I could read my books and continue my studies. Every other day, I'd ride my motorcycle to Sarnath to study with my Tibetan teachers, and each week, I began new conversations with learned Indian philosophers and spiritual teachers. Very quickly, I realized how silly my aversion to Varanasi had been. Still, I just couldn't seem to feel happy about being there. Finally, it occurred to me that it was time for the rubber of my meditation to meet the road of ordinary life. In other words, my meditations could no longer be just a pleasant respite from life's realities, but an integral preparation for the whole of life. After all, my Tibetan teachers exhibited extraordinary countenance, compassion, and cheerfulness, despite the unbearable hardships of refugee life in India—not to mention the loss of their homeland, their families, and their monasteries. Why shouldn't I be able to do it?

So I began an experiment in my morning meditations to see if I could develop some mental contentment and gratitude about dwelling in this place so foreign to my natural sensibilities. I needed to connect the dots between the peace, tranquility, and insights from meditation and everyday life in a strange land.

At the outset of each day, before doing anything else, I experimented with transitioning from sleeping and dreaming directly into meditating. I would move through the stages of meditation as I had been trained, but at the conclusion of each morning meditation, I would bring to mind all the disturbing aspects of Varanasi that I would face that day—the people, the traffic, the noise, the jostle, the pollution—and apply the tranquility, compassion, and insight from my meditation to each of these. In other words, the people, events, and circumstances of the coming day would become the new focus of the last stage of my meditation.

I would expand and infuse my meditations on breathing, mindfulness, emptiness, gratitude, forgiveness, love and compassion into each element of the coming day. I attempted to equalize my compassion for everyone, whether I liked them or not. I attempted to bring equanimity into every situation, whether I chose it or not. Therefore, the benediction for each morning meditation was an extension and infusion of this consciousness into all aspects of the day's realities, pleasant and unpleasant. In effect, I was learning how to 'pre-load' my meditation state into all the events, circumstances, and relationships of the coming day.

The result of this experiment was a dramatic change in my state of mind. Each day I was renewed with a sense of contentment, tranquility, and gratitude for my life in Varanasi. This personal experiment with meditation showed me that I—indeed all of us—have the capacity to change, adapt, and flourish in difficult circumstances. Since then, I have also learned how many of the world's contemplative traditions have similar methods for integrating meditation and prayer into daily life. So it is clear to me that we must close our meditation with a fierce dedication— an unrelenting determination—to bring our contemplative Motivation, Gratitude, Transformation, Compassion, Mindfulness, and Meditation into our daily lives. This is the central purpose for our human existence, and therefore, the final stage of InterSpiritual Meditation.

SEALING THE DEAL

At this point in the process, we 'seal the deal' and dedicate the merit of all that we have done for the happiness of all beings.[70] The "deal" is the agreement we have made with ourselves in the previous steps: to become healthy and happy, to live gratefully, to transform ourselves, to be compassionate, to be mindful, and to meditate on the profound truths of our existence—all for the larger purpose of infusing the world with compassion, peace, and wisdom. To this end, we dedicate the benefits of our meditation. That is to say, whatever we have gained in meditation is dedicated to the health, happiness, transformation, and freedom of all beings, not just our own selfish health and happiness.

This dedication is the logical conclusion of our understanding that each thought, word, and action is a seed planted in our consciousness, just waiting to ripen in the future. The quality of the fruit depends on the motivation, intention, and dedication with which the seed was planted. Therefore, for our meditation to have the greatest possible effect in the world, it is imperative that each meditative session end with a dedication, with the planting of a great intentional seed.

The law of causality states: everything that happens has an effect on the future; and since our thoughts, words, and actions are all accompanied by motivations and intentions, these must also condition the future result. If our intention for meditation is only for short-term results—say, for immediate peace of mind and to restore calm—we might achieve these; but as soon as these fade, we will need to 'refuel the tank' with another meditative session.

However, if our intention and motivation is adjusted for the long-term—say, for the eternal happiness and enlightenment of all beings—then our 'fuel reservoir' will grow to accommodate the scale of our intentions. Likewise, if we seek eternal liberation and happiness for all beings, in all times and places, the corresponding reservoir and benefits grow to infinite dimensions. Simply put, the effect of our meditation is proportional to the cause; the more profound the intention, the more profound the result. So one's dedication at the end of a period of meditation should speak of one's highest ideals and best intentions.

It is also important to understand that, just as the depth and quality of our meditation depends on the sincerity of our compassionate intention, our ability to help others after meditation depends on the sincerity of our closing dedication. That is to say, it is not enough merely to state our ideals; it must be a true intention, meaning that we intend to participate in making it happen. For it doesn't do the world much good if we believe in peace and harmony, and then continue to sow the seeds of discord with a discordant state of mind. According to the principles of spiritual psychology, the quality and benefit of our subsequent actions is proportional to the purity of our original intention and dedication. Simply put, our own happiness is dependent on the sincerity of our dedication to help others.

Therefore, at the close of our meditation session, it is important to emerge slowly from the meditative state and to gather ourselves for a moment before making our dedication with fully conscious intention. This allows us to transition back into the realm of sensation and worldly activity, gradually, with a clear and renewed purpose. It is a mistake—and a jolt to our psyche—if we suddenly rise from meditation and to rush back into the chaos of the everyday world. So be sure to take a few minutes, allowing the tranquil and healing energy of your meditation to flow through you, to permeate every cell of your body before you fully re-enter the stream of sensory consciousness. This energetic flow will remain with you throughout your day and provide you with strength of compassion and wisdom for yourself as well as for others. As you are filled with altruistic love and healing energy, you should feel both a personal renewal and a renewed purpose to bring love and compassion into the world, and to alleviate the suffering of all beings.

At the close of your meditation, you might feel a sense of calm, or perhaps even a light tingling of energy circulating from your head to your toes, in the tips of your fingers and throughout your entire body. Try to imagine this as a radiant energy of love being transferred to the entire world.

EXTENSION & PERSEVERANCE

Our task as we leave the meditation space is to gradually transfer this energy of love outward, so that all beings can benefit from our experience of intimacy with the most profound aspects of our being. As we do so, we can feel our consciousness spreading outward, bringing peace and a healing energy into the consciousness of all beings, everywhere. Without pretence, we humbly send these qualities into the hearts and minds of those around us, and then throughout our neighborhoods, towns, regions, states, countries, hemispheres, and the whole world, the solar system, and the entire universe. We visualize and feel the light, love, wisdom, and peace experienced in our own meditation being infused into all beings, everywhere.

Then we set before our eyes the daily flow of our own specific lives, and the faces of the real people and activities of our everyday world. We bring to mind specific people or situations with which we have had difficulties. Using the tools of our meditative session, we re-orientate the nature of our relationships with these people. We transform the negative emotions that we previously brought into these situations by applying the tools of compassion that we cultivated in Step Four of our process.

In the light generated by our meditative experience, we begin to reformulate the way we will be in relationship with difficult people and situations. We recall past interactions that were difficult, perhaps even painful, allowing ourselves to feel some of the fears, anger, or frustration we might have felt at the time. Then we see ourselves through the eyes of 'the other,' imagining the internal causes for their difficulty with us, identifying with their own difficult life-circumstances that may have caused them to react negatively toward us.

Now, with the wisdom, love, and compassion generated in our meditation, we intentionally reformulate our way of being in the world in order to help everyone we meet during the coming day.

We need to be patient and forgiving of ourselves in this process of transformation, for it will take time to adjust to a new way of being in relationship with difficult people and challenging situations. Nevertheless, this final step of our meditation process will gradually transform the frame of reference for these challenging relationships.

Before arising from meditation, we imagine the predictable situations of our day and bring to mind the normal stress-points of everyday life. We make a promise to bring our contemplative intentions, ideals, and epiphanies into these situations, to regard these challenges with gratitude rather than resentment. For these are gifts that can help us deepen, refine, and extend our wisdom and compassion in the world. These difficult situations are the foundation for growth and evolution.

This infusion of our spiritual reality into our worldly activities should be seen as a natural extension and practical conclusion to this time we have spent alone with ourselves, establishing a compassionate framework for the rest of our day. As we complete this session of meditation, remember that the intention of our meditation is to become compassionate participants in the world, not to withdraw in isolation and self-protection from the world.

Finally, let us make an internal pact with ourselves to persevere in meditation each and every day of our lives. For only through a lived practice of engaged contemplation and meditation can we hope to achieve sustained peace, happiness, and fulfillment for our selves and our loved-ones throughout the world. Visualizing our family, friends, enemies, colleagues, and all beings, we vow to help alleviate suffering and achieve sustainable love, peace and happiness. May this meditation help us to go forth and engage the world with wisdom and compassion.

So let us make this silent vow . . .

*"May I Serve All Beings with Compassion, Peace, and Wisdom"*

*The Lord bless you and keep you;*
*The Lord deal kindly and graciously with you;*
*The Lord bestow favor on you and give you peace.*
*— TaNaK, Numbers, 6:24-26*

# PART III
## RESOURCES FOR
## INTERSPIRITUAL MEDITATION

# INTRODUCTION

PART THREE has two main sections: the first contains general advice on the practice of InterSpiritual Meditation, choosing a spiritual tradition and teacher, meditative postures and the proper environment for meditation; the second contains meditations from six different traditions and teachers. These meditations include a Buddhist *shamatha* and *vipashyana* by myself, the Christian Centering Prayer practice as taught by Father Thomas Keating, a Hindu *pranayama* meditation by Yogi Nataraja Kallio, a Sufi Islamic breath meditation on the elements by Pir Zia Inayat-Khan, a Jewish meditation on breathing the divine name by Rabbi Jeff Roth, and a Taoist meditation practice by Ken Cohen. This section is just a preview of our companion volume, *Meditations for InterSpiritual Practice,* which contains many more practices from the world's contemplative traditions.

As we contemplate these meditative prescriptions, we begin to taste the marvelous diversity of practices among the world's spiritual heritage. Over the millennia, their ingredients have been shared, and yet each has distinctive qualities that are essential to them. Refined discernment is essential lest we misappropriate the practices of one into another. For each practice is founded on a lineage of teachings passed down from teacher to student for hundreds of generations. They encapsulate metaphysical, ethical, cultural, and mystical subtleties that can only be known through formation within the tradition, and with teachers and mentors who can lead us one step at a time, always making sure that our foundation is strong enough to support these practices.

In the InterSpiritual work of the Spiritual Paths Foundation, we honor the marvelous variety of views and practice. We try to avoid the temptation to claim that "all religions are . . ." because the subtle variations defy facile generalizations. We take great care in speaking for each other's traditions, for we know the depth of experience and training required to do so with integrity. To teach without proper training is to trivialize the tradition of which we speak. Although mature contemplatives of all traditions have widely diverse personalities they are united by a compassionate intent and an internal wisdom that guides their being in the world.

When we practice our various forms of meditation together in shared silence, the emergence of a distinctive InterSpiritual Consciousness is palpable. This deeply shared experience is the foundation for the harmony and common commitment to heal the wounds of human beings and nature.

# BEGINNING YOUR INTERSPIRITUAL
# MEDITATION PRACTICE

THE EXPERIENCE AT THE SNOWMASS CONFERENCE, which I described in Chapter 3 ("The Process of InterSpiritual Meditation"), was truly critical for me. It showed me a possibility I had never considered before—that people of different faiths could come together to share an experience of profound spiritual depth. During that silent meditation, which included a Hindu swami of the Vedanta tradition, an Eastern Orthodox Christian priest, a Hasidic Jew, and a Muslim Sufi, it was clear to me that a group consciousness was being created by us, even in the silence.[71] It is this consciousness that I now tend to think of as an InterSpiritual Consciousness. Let me give you an example that may hit a little closer to home:

Imagine you are in a room with a group of angry people, perhaps a tension filled boardroom, or in an airport terminal when your flight has just been cancelled. Is it really necessary to say anything for the anger and frustration to be communicated? We have all been in these situations, and we all know that the group-feeling is communicated, even without words. This is why we say things like, 'You could cut the tension with a knife,' because the feeling is almost tangible.

Likewise, there are shared environments of excitement, as at sporting events and concerts, joy and love in gatherings of friends and family, inexplicable empathy between strangers in times of danger; but we don't generally consider the implications of this sharing. We take it for granted, which is to say that we participate in these 'sharings' unconsciously. But what if we didn't? What if we gathered together with the conscious intention of cultivating love and harmony through a shared experience of group meditation? What if people of different faiths could join together in an all-inclusive meditation process? Is it possible that something might be shared between them, a new and deeper intimacy created? I believe this is precisely what can result.[72]

If the sensitivity of our individual consciousness is not confined to particular parts of our bodies, if it extends in some way beyond our bodies, and further, if in meditation we all simultaneously give rise to a shared intention, isn't it possible then that individual consciousness may conjoin with the consciousness of other individuals to form a larger group consciousness? As I said before, this idea was a "breakthrough" for me, but not because I hadn't already experienced this in meditation and practice with other Buddhists, but because I had never considered it possible with people of different faiths! The truth is, many spiritual traditions have long been aware of and have even cultivated group consciousness, but not many have extended it to the sharing of intentions *InterSpiritually,* that is to say, with persons of other faiths, as we are beginning to do today.

Nor was this a breakthrough for me alone, or else I might be suspected of fooling myself. But some of my other colleagues at the Snowmass Conference had experienced the same phenomenon. It was something that happened in the silence of shared periods of meditation and subsequent dialogues, something pointed out by Father Keating and repeated by Swami Atmarupananda in the book *The Common Heart:*

> [W]hen the dialogue [following our meditation] is good, we share an experience of flowing with a higher intelligence; our individual understanding seems uplifted into a collective sharing with something higher. That is how Father Tom [Keating] expressed it in our last meeting. In a sense, this is the most important aspect of dialogue. It doesn't always happen, but when it does, there is nothing like it. When we are immersed in the wisdom of the collective sharing, a higher understanding descends on all of the individuals.[73]

The "dialogue" Father Keating and Swami Atmarupananda are talking about is not merely the verbal dialogue of our group discussion sessions, but also that of our silent meditations together. This is what we called, "the silent dialogue," which was every bit as enriching as the group discussions.[74] Indeed, one participant, a Calvinist Christian minister, Rev. Don Postema, said of one of our silent meditation sessions:

> There was truly a profound connection without words. And I remember that during one of those silent sessions in Cohasset

[Massachusetts, where the seventh Snowmass Conference took place], I had a profound experience of the Presence of Jesus; my own experience of Christianity was strengthened through sharing meditation with folks of different spiritual traditions![75]

From this we can also see that even as we join together to create a group consciousness, individual experiences of profound depth are not hindered, and may even be enhanced. This is an important part of the InterSpiritual Meditation process, for even as we are sharing the process itself, and even as we may be creating a group consciousness, we are still using the language and basic practices of our own traditions. Thus, highly unique insights may occur and one may become more deeply grounded in one's own tradition.

Keep this in mind as you begin your practice of InterSpiritual Meditation. Though you may be starting your exploration of this process alone, or for your own personal development, look for opportunities to share it with others, especially those who may be pursuing different spiritual paths, or doing different meditation techniques. For the sharing of an InterSpiritual Consciousness is a major purpose of this process, and the means by which we may help to bring a little more peace to our fractured world.

GETTING STARTED

So how does one begin a meditation practice? Obviously, we need to start small and begin at the beginning. After all, what mathematician ever started out with Calculus? First there was simple addition and subtraction, then division, then the multiplication tables. These are the foundations upon which the future mathematician builds their knowledge, gradually increasing their skill and competence in applying them year after year.

Of course, meditation does not require so much preliminary knowledge, but a mature meditation practice does take time to develop and has certain basic features that must be understood first. Like any other discipline, meditation takes dedication, time, patience, and work in order to bear fruit. Therefore, I want to discuss the context in which meditation is usually done, and some of the preliminaries to meditation practice.

## Spiritual Traditions and Teachers

If you do not have a particular meditation practice, or do not belong to an established spiritual tradition, it might be helpful to explore the various meditation resources in this section of the book. However, if you are actively looking for a path or a teacher, I would encourage you to use the utmost discretion and discernment in making this decision. Take your time and allow yourself to think it through thoroughly. As long as this isn't an avoidance tactic (or a habitual fear of commitment), diligence and perspicacity are advisable. Your spiritual future depends on making good and thoughtful decisions.[1]

Once you have made an informed decision about your path, it is equally important to stay focused within a specific tradition until you have learned it well. Then you will be better prepared to explore the different aspects of meditation in other traditions. Although meditation practices across traditions share many basic features, there are also important nuances to their presentation and practice that can have a profound impact on the meditator. Keep this in mind as you explore the practices provided here.

Spiritual traditions are more than just their meditation practices; they are entire 'cultures' with unique rituals and customs, approaches and beliefs, and very particular paths to human transformation. So as you explore, try to do so as a traveler entering an indigenous village, treading carefully and with respect, approaching everything with 'beginner's mind.'

Why should you have a meditation teacher? Like many other life disciplines, it is helpful to refine our knowledge and practice by working with a good teacher within a well-established tradition. Meditation can be a long, slow process, and it is valuable to have someone with whom we can check our progress—and sometimes, our fantasies. Occasionally we cling to fantastic experiences that arise in our meditation and try to repeat these experiences again and again. While these experiences can be enthralling, they are often just distractions, the illusory projections of our own minds. It is also possible that you might have an experience that is unsettling and disorienting. A good teacher can let you know when you are on the right track, and help you to find balance and perspective again after potentially destabilizing experiences.

With regard to teachers, a great Hindu swami once said to me,

"Because it is the disciple who must determine the 'guruness' of the guru, the disciple is actually the guru of the guru." One of my own teachers, Geshe Sopa, occasionally quoted the Buddha who said something along these lines: 'Don't put all your trust in the charisma of a teacher, but judge their living example. Still, don't have faith in this example alone, but pay attention to the wisdom of their words. Don't focus on the surface meaning of the words, but examine their deeper meaning. And don't stop your inquiry with the apparent or explicit meaning, but contemplate deeply the hidden or implicit meaning."

Geshe Sopa also quoted another saying of the Buddha as well: "Don't take my teachings on faith; rather, you should test the meanings like a goldsmith who assays the quality of the gold. You should rub it, cut it, burn it, and taste it." Faith based on a thorough discernment is more durable, and more sustainable. In the end, each of us must authenticate and actualize the teachings of any tradition through our own experience.

POSTURES *&* ENVIRONMENT

It is helpful to create an environment and maintain a body posture that is conducive for meditation. Before beginning the InterSpiritual Meditation process, you may want to light a candle or burn some incense to honor the beginning of the session. You should take a posture that is at once comfortable and stable; this might be cross-legged on a cushion on the floor, or on a chair with your back straight (not rigid) and your feet flat on the floor. Often, various meditative traditions have their own recommended postures; if you are not aware of them, these instructions will do fine for now. You might want to place your hands gently on your lap, or simply palms down on the tops of your thighs, roughly equidistant between your hip-joint and knees. You should feel relaxed within your body and fully present in this place.

At this point, you might adjust your gaze downward, gently closing your eyes until there is just a thin crack of light coming in. Begin inhaling and exhaling softly and evenly through your nose. Place the tip of your tongue on the roof of your mouth just behind your upper front teeth while your lips are kept gently together. Breathing easily, simply relax into the silence.

Lastly, you might want to place a small clock near your downward gaze so you can time your session. The seven parts of the InterSpiritual Meditation process outlined below have individual recommended time increments for a thirty-minute session of meditation.

## SOLO & GROUP PRACTICE

The seven-part process of InterSpiritual Meditation provides a framework for individual and group practice. If you are using this process to guide an InterSpiritual group of meditators, I encourage you to begin the sessions together with a minimum of words. Let the shared silence be the connecting medium between you. Likewise, as you enter each individual step of the process, introduce that step with just a few words that indicate the purpose of the next few minutes, or with an experienced group who knows the process, you might simply use a small bell or gong to indicate the movement from one step to the next.

If you are doing this practice on your own, in the beginning it might be useful to follow the process in the order and time sequence in which it is presently arranged. Then, once you are familiar with each of the elements, you might customize it according to your own preferences. My goal is not to proscribe a rigid dogma, but to lay out the elements of a mature process for you to experience, experiment with, and integrate into your own personal practice.

## THE INTERSPIRITUAL MEDITATION PROCESS

The following is an outline of the seven steps and suggested times for each part of the process with simplified verbal indications you might use in leading a group or in teaching yourself the process:

### 1.   Step One – Motivation (3 Minutes)
*"May I Be Healthy and Happy"*

In order to achieve anything significant in our lives—whether in our careers, sports, or relationships—we must have the proper motivation. Likewise, a lifelong spiritual practice also requires strong and unwavering motivation. In this first step, we establish our motivation and prayers for physical, emotional, mental, and spiritual healing, leading to sustainable happiness. To help us persevere, we begin each session by contemplating our own personal reasons and experiences that have brought us here.

    *a. Mind*
    *b. Body*
    *c. Spirit*

2.  *Step Two – Gratitude (3 Minutes)*
*"May I Be Grateful for Life's Many Gifts"*

There is so much for which we can be grateful: our environment that gives us life and sustains us, life's challenges that enable us to grow, to become compassionate and wise, our ancestors and loved ones, our teachers and mentors. Whenever we learn to perform a new task, we depend on the example of others to guide us. This is especially true in spiritual practice when we invoke, remember, and honor the presence of our teachers, mentors, the saints, prophets, and founders of our respective traditions, and not least, God or the sacred dimension. We visualize and invite them to join us; we pray for their help that we might help others; and we thank them for all they have done for us. In this step, we can express gratitude for life's great challenges through which we gain the wisdom and compassion to help others. We can give thanks to the natural world that sustains us. We can invoke the infinite potential that lies within our own consciousness, a potential for wisdom, compassion, and health. We invoke these with deep gratitude. Here are some of the attributes to be contemplated and cultivated in your journaling and meditation sessions.

    *a. Remembrance*
    *b. Gratitude*
    *c. Trust*
    *d. Devotion*
    *e. Prayer*
    *f. Offering*

3.  *Step Three – Transformation (3 Minutes)*
*"May I Be Transformed Into My Highest Ideal"*

In order to improve ourselves—whether professionally, in academics, athletics, ethics, in relationships, or spiritually—we must develop a clear image of that which we would like to become. Then we must be honest about our present condition, giving ourselves a personal 'reality check' with regard to our present inadequacies and the ways in which we would like to improve. We must admit that there is something wrong, something unsatisfactory in our lives, areas that we would like to improve, and make a promise to ourselves that we will strive to transform ourselves into the beings we most sincerely want to become. Without investing in debilitating guilt, we forgive ourselves (and others) for any part we (or they) might have played in our present situation. We love the wounded parts of ourselves, the negative emotions and bad habits that need healing and transformation. We renounce our attachment to the habits, desires, and behaviors that do not serve our highest ideals. Finally, we open ourselves to love, the universal healing and transformative agent for all beings everywhere. We are now ready to embark on the meditative practices required to acquire the qualities we desire and to eliminate the obstacles in our path. Here are some of the attributes to be contemplated and cultivated in your journaling and meditation sessions.

> *a. Visualizing the Ideal*
> *b. Honest Self-Assessment*
> *c. Confession*
> *d. Remorse*
> *e. Inward Love*
> *f. Forgiveness*
> *g. Surrender*
> *h. Commitment*

## 4. Step Four – Compassion (3 Minutes)

### "May I Be Loving and Compassionate"

Practically speaking, love and compassion for others are the foundation stones for our own happiness and well-being. They are the universal currency of reciprocity between all beings, and the fundamental values that lie at the heart of all spiritual traditions. At this stage in our meditation process, we allow ourselves to be infused and immersed in the presence of universal love. We radiate love and compassion to all beings, including ourselves—love that spontaneously wishes happiness for all beings, and the compassion that constantly strives to remove the causes of their suffering. We vow to dedicate our lives to this loving and compassionate intention. Here are some of the attributes to be contemplated and cultivated in your journaling and meditation sessions.

> *a. Exchanging Self for Others*
> *b. Existential Reciprocity*
> *c. Universal Love*

## 5. Step Five – Mindfulness (5 Minutes)
### "May I Be Focused and Mindful Through Breathing"

Calm, steady, and focused breathing are at the heart of many secular and spiritual techniques of meditation. When we breathe properly, we become less stressed and distracted; we are able to think more clearly, and to focus on the task at hand. Our blood-pressure drops, and our anxiety disappears. Many spiritual traditions teach deep and profound methods of breathing that balance our energies and center our consciousness deep within our being, where we are able to concentrate on our spiritual practice. In this step, we allow our consciousness to recede from our eyes, ears, nose, tongue, touch, thoughts, and emotions. As we breathe gently, our consciousness rides on the subtle breath into our heart center. This is the place that many traditions call 'the seat of the soul,' the core of our consciousness. Residing there, we may begin our own respective meditations, contemplations, and prayers. In this process, we learn to develop the capacity of 'mindfulness' and to observe our innermost thoughts, emotions, habits, and memories. Here are some of the attributes to be contemplated and cultivated in your journaling and meditation sessions.

> *a. Body Position*
> *b. Focus on the Subtle Breath*
> *c. Concentration and Attention*
> *d. Recollection*

*e. Observation and Vigilance*
*f. Patience*
*g. Perseverance*
*h. Quiescence*

## 6. Step Six – Meditation (10 Minutes)

### "May I Become Wise Through Meditation"

Now that the garden of our mind has been carefully cultivated, we can begin to deepen and expand the scope of our meditation. Honoring the profound and marvelous diversity among the world's contemplative traditions, we silently engage in the meditation of our own tradition or choosing, opening to transcendent insight, deep tranquility, or unity with that which is sacred to us. Mindful breathing itself can remain our sole focus or may provide a foundation for our chosen meditation. (See the various practices given below.) Here are some of the attributes to be contemplated and cultivated in your journaling and meditation sessions.

*a. Tranquil Focus*
*b. Insight*
*c. Equanimity*
*d. Unity*
*e. Absorption*
*f. Transcendence*

## 7. Step Seven – Dedication (3 Minutes)

### "May I Serve All Beings with Compassion, Peace, and Wisdom"

In order for our meditation to have power in our lives and benefit others, we must rededicate ourselves to our loving and compassionate intentions. May our meditation help us to engage in the world with wisdom and compassion. As we visualize our family, friends, enemies, colleagues, communities, and beings throughout the world, we vow to help alleviate their suffering and achieve sustainable love, peace and happiness for all.

Before you arise engage in the following:

*a. Vow to keep this meditation in the background of your mind throughout the day.*
*b. Visualize the events, situations and people that will be challenging.*
*c. Infuse each of these challenging moments with your insights with this meditation*

In group practice, when the meditation is over and you emerge from silence together, you might find that your subsequent dialogue may reveal exhilarating new insights and bring you closer together. As Father Keating often says: "silence is the first language of the Divine, or that which we might call God. Let us share in this silent communication before using words."

This meditation should be entered into with gentle compassion. At first, the discipline may be difficult, like starting a new exercise regime. But as with exercise, you may begin to see short-term results fairly quickly, though the more permanent, long-term changes will take time and perseverance. Like any other worthwhile life-venture, we need to be prepared to stick with the training and preparation required to fully reap the results. That is why it is so important to keep ourselves motivated. We should continually remind ourselves that these seven steps need to be practiced each day of our lives.

Finally, I strongly recommend that you keep a journal of your intentions for each of the seven steps. Each of these can yield profound inner guidance for all aspects of your life. There is an intimate and interdependent relationship between the quality of your daily life, your nighttime dreaming, and your meditations. Your journal will provide you with focal points for the actual meditation sessions and it will chart the progress of your contemplative journey through life.

# A Selection of
# Meditations from
# Various Traditions

The following meditations are prescribed by exemplars
of six of the world's great spiritual traditions.

# CULTIVATING TRANQUIL FOCUS & TRANSCENDENTAL INSIGHT

## Edward W. Bastian

THE LIFE STORY of the Buddha has resonance for all of us who are compelled to discover the truth of our existence and the path to eternal happiness. For here was a human being endowed with every possible material and sensual pleasure, and yet, these could not satisfy his longing. So he set off on a lonely and difficult journey to discover the truth of all existence and the source of happiness. And throughout history, countless people have been inspired to do the same by the Buddha's heroic example.

The Buddha studied with the great teachers of his time and experienced the fruit of their practices: he experimented with extreme austerity; he begged for food; he absorbed the major metaphysical teachings of India, meditating on the possible unity of his individual soul *(atman)* with the ultimate universal creator *(Brahman);* and he nearly died of starvation for fear of harming other living beings. Finally, he decided to simply sit beneath a tree until the truth emerged. After forty-nine days and nights of meditating he experienced the omniscience of enlightenment, liberation from the causes of suffering, and the bliss of *Nirvana.* For the next forty-five years, he taught others to experience this for themselves and laid the foundation for one of the world's great spiritual traditions.

Based on his own experience, he concluded that everyone had the potential to see the true nature of existence, to achieve eternal enlightenment and bliss, and to help others achieve the same goals. But doing this would require a skillful combination of wisdom and compassionate service.

The Buddha found that the cause of our suffering is our attachment to the notion of an independent, unchanging soul, and the idea that the objects we perceive exist independently, causing us to see them as other than they are. We mistakenly believe that these objects are intrinsically desirable or undesirable, and therefore, have the power to make us happy or sad. To heal us of this misperception, the Buddha taught us that that things and people are impermanent, interdependent, and empty of inherent existence.

It is only our own ignorance, desire, and attachment that causes things to be desirable and undesirable, beautiful and ugly. People and things don't cause us to see them as good or bad. Rather, we impose that judgment on them. We project our ignorance and emotions on them, and this causes us to be in a state of anxiety, emotional unrest, and suffering.

How do we stop this incessant projection? How do we stop clinging to our judgments about people and things? How do we come to grips with the fact that the external word is not what it seems to be? How do we recondition our mind to see things as they are, and to behave compassionately towards others?

For the Buddha, the answer is meditation. In the *Satipatthana Sutta,* which contains some of his earliest teachings, it says:

> [T]his is the direct path for the purification of beings, for the surmounting of sorrow and lamentation, for the disappearance of *dukkha* [suffering] and discontent, for acquiring the true method, for the realizations of *Nibbana [Nirvana],* namely, the four *satipatthanas* [true foundations].
>
> What are the four? Here, [. . .] in regard to the body (feelings, mind, *dhammas* [phenomena]) a [meditator] abides contemplating the body, diligent, clearly knowing, and mindful, free from desires and discontent in regard to the world.

Here, the Buddha is teaching us to focus our attention solely on our body, feelings, mind, and all existents. This tranquil, undistracted focus is called *shamatha,* and it is the first step toward Mindfulness. *Shamatha* training begins by cultivating a calm, single-pointed focus on the constituents of our being and the objects of our perception.

*Shamatha* generally begins with undistracted attention to breathing. Then, once our mind is calm and undistracted, we can shift our attention to other aspects of the body like our posture, movements, anatomical parts, elements, and even our future corpse in decay. Once we have completed a *shamatha*-scan of our body, we focus on our feelings, our mind, and everything that we perceive *(dhammas)*. *Shamatha* can be practiced while sitting, standing, walking, or lying down. It enables us to be exquisitely aware of all aspects of our being and to attune our words, thoughts, and actions to our compassionate intention for living. It is the foundational practice of many Buddhist meditations.

*Shamatha* or Mindfulness meditation can have wondrous effects on the body and mind. It can quell stress, anxiety, hypertension, high blood pressure, and help cure the myriad diseases that stem from these. It is also said to give way to a range of psychic abilities, including clairvoyance. But it is just the first step along the Buddhist path of meditation. For as the 8th-century Buddhist teacher Kamalasila said in his "Stages of Meditation":

Yogis cannot eliminate mental obscurations merely by familiarizing themselves with calm abiding meditation alone. It will only suppress the disturbing emotions and delusions temporarily. Without the light of wisdom, the latent potential of the disturbing emotions cannot be thoroughly destroyed, and therefore their complete destruction will not be possible.

Knowing this, the Buddha provided us with further instructions in the *Satipatthana Sutta:*

He abides contemplating the nature of both the arising and passing away in the body (feelings, mind, *dhammas).* Mindfulness that 'there is a body' is established in him to the extent necessary for bare knowledge and continuous mindfulness. And he abides independent, not clinging to anything in the world.

Here, the Buddha instructs us on the second phase of meditation called *vipashyana,* often translated as 'transcendental insight.' At this stage in the meditation, having employed *shamatha* to focus on an object (or a category meditational objects), the meditator applies analytical wisdom to that object. This is the wisdom that knows all phenomena to be constantly "rising and passing away." It knows that all phenomena are interdependent and conditioned by the projections of the mind that perceives them. Or, as the Buddhist philosopher Nagarjuna stated it in his "Seventy Verses on Emptiness":

> All things arise from causes and conditions;
> To view them as real is ignorance;
> From this arises the twelve interdependent links.

One of the Buddha's unique contributions to our global spiritual heritage is his proposition that liberation gradually emerges by eliminating the causes of our bondage. Truth and freedom naturally arise once we eliminate the ignorance, attachment, and desire that cloud our minds. Having removed the clouds, we are able to perceive the true nature of reality. Based on this wisdom we are truly able to serve others.

The combination of *shamatha* and *vipashyana* are designed to eliminate the obstacles to our enlightenment. The following passage from the "Heart Sutra" takes this a step further. Here, in addition to seeing just the "rising and falling away" of all phenomena, we are instructed to see that all things are also "empty of intrinsic existence":

> Shariputra, a noble son or noble daughter who so wishes to engage in the practice of the profound perfection of wisdom should clearly see this way: They should see perfectly that even the five aggregates are empty of intrinsic existence. Form is emptiness, emptiness is form. Emptiness is not other than form, form too is not other than emptiness. Likewise, feelings, perceptions, mental formations, and consciousness are all empty.

Here we are taught to hold each of the five aggregates (form, feelings, perceptions, mental formations, and consciousness) as the objects of *shamatha* meditation, and then through *vipashyana* meditation, to directly perceive the fact that they are empty of intrinsic existence. 'Emptiness of intrinsic of existence' is a negative way or saying that all phenomena are impermanent and interdependent. That is, things are 'empty' of the capacity of existing permanently, intrinsically, and independently. The meditative laser-beam of emptiness dissolves our ignorance, desire, and attachment, thus freeing our minds to see things as they really are.

So we see that *shamatha* and *vipashyana* remain the consistent meditative thread through many types of Buddhist meditation. This combination of tranquil focus and transcendental insight is meant to help us to experience the very same realization as the Buddha had, to shed clinging and attachment to projected illusions, and to experience the bliss and liberation that comes when our mind is purified.

As the great master Shantideva says in Chapter 8 of his "Way of the Bodhisattva":

*Cultivating diligence as just described,*
*In concentration I will place my mind.*
*For those whose minds are slack and wandering*
*Are caught between the fangs of the afflictions.*

*In solitude, the mind and body*
*Are not troubled by distraction.*
*Therefore leave this worldly life*
*And totally abandon mental wandering.*

*Because of loved ones and desire for gain,*
*We fail to turn away from worldly things.*
*These, then, are the first things to renounce.*
*The prudent should conduct themselves like this.*

*Penetrative insight joined with calm abiding*
*Utterly eradicates afflicted states.*
*Knowing this, first search for calm abiding,*
*Found by people who are happy to be free from worldly ties.*

SHAMATHA AND VIPASHYANA:
A SAMPLE MEDITATION SESSION

We assume a relaxed, meditative posture in a quiet spot where distractions and interruptions are minimal.

Then, we set our intention thus: May this meditation generate wisdom to help others to be enlightened and free from suffering.

We begin our *shamatha* meditation by focusing our attention on the breath. For the next few minutes, we concentrate solely on the feeling of the air caressing the entrance of our nostrils.

We allow our whole body to relax and feel the tranquility of one-pointed attention on our breathing. We gently breathe-in for six seconds, hold our breath for four seconds, and exhale for six seconds. We find our own natural rhythm for breathing.

We imagine our conscious awareness riding on this smooth, subtle stream of air as it travels through our nasal passages, down the back of our throat, into our lungs, and expanding out to the extremities of our chest. We feel the oxygen flowing to every living cell in our body.

Simultaneously, from the background of our mind, we watch for any distracting sounds, sensations, thoughts, memories, and daydreams. We let our "mental spy" keep a look out from the background of our consciousness. When it spots an incoming distraction, we simply name it—a sound, an image, a memory, a sensation—and let it dissolve like a cloud dissipating into the blue sky.

This calm focus on breathing is the beginning stage of shamatha meditation. For the next few minutes, we keep our attention solely on the breath as it enters and circulates throughout our entire system.

Next, we engage the *vipashyana* phase of our meditation. Keeping tranquil focus, we observe how our breath rises and falls away. We observe the impermanence and the interdependence of breathing. For example, we observe how breathing-in the oxygen from the earth's plants nourishes the trillions of living the cells of our body. We observe how our out-breath of carbon dioxide nourishes these plants in turn. We become fully absorbed in the interdependent reciprocity of being.

Finally, we observe how our breath is empty, our bodily cells are empty, how all phenomena are empty of permanence and intrinsic existence. We become fully absorbed in this insight about the emptiness of all phenomena.

In this way, the insight of our *vipashyana* meditation

rests on the tranquil focus of our *shamatha* meditation. They become two essential components a single meditative session. Gradually, we apply these to our body, feelings, mind, and all phenomena that appear in our consciousness. In so doing, our calm and compassionate wisdom flourishes along with the profound fulfillment of serving others.

# FINDING INTIMACY WITH GOD

## *Father Thomas Keating*

CENTERING PRAYER is a method of silent prayer that is designed to deepen our relationship with Christ and to prepare us to receive the gift of contemplative prayer, prayer in which we experience God's presence within us, closer than our very breath, closer than our thoughts, closer than consciousness itself; it is both a relationship with God and a discipline to foster that relationship.

The method itself was developed by Father William Meninger in the mid-1970's and based on indications from the anonymous Christian spiritual classic, The Cloud of Unknowing. Today it is practiced by people all over the world and spread through the work of Contemplative Outreach. Centering Prayer is not meant to replace other kinds of prayer; it simply adds depth of meaning to them, and to our daily lives. Centering Prayer is a movement beyond conversation with Christ to communion with Him, to a silent resting in His loving Presence.

## THE METHOD OF CENTERING PRAYER

*1. Choose a sacred word as the symbol of your intention to consent to God's presence and action within.*

This word expresses our intention to be in God's presence and to yield to the divine action. It should be chosen during a brief period of prayer asking the Holy Spirit to inspire us with one that is especially suitable for us. Examples of this word might be: 'Lord,' 'Jesus,' 'Abba,' 'Father,' 'Mother,' or even, 'Love,' 'Peace,' 'Shalom,' or 'Silence.' Whatever word you choose, it should be used for the entire period of prayer.

*2. Sitting comfortably and with eyes closed, settle briefly, and silently introduce the sacred word as the symbol of your consent to God's presence and action within.*

"Sitting comfortably" does not mean that we are so comfortable that we might fall asleep, but just comfortable enough to avoid thinking about the discomfort of our bodies during prayer. Keeping one's back straight is an important part of proper posture for Centering Prayer. We also close our eyes in this process to let go of what is going on around us. For it is into this withdrawal from the senses that we introduce the sacred word, as gently as laying a feather on a piece of absorbent cotton.

*3. When you become aware of being engaged with your thoughts, return ever-so-gently to the sacred word.*

"Thoughts" may refer to any perception, including sense perceptions, feelings, images, memories, reflections, and commentaries. It is normal for these perceptions to arise, but still we should remember to return "ever-so-gently to the sacred word," using the minimum of effort. This is the only activity we initiate during the time of Centering Prayer. However, during the course of your prayer, you may notice that the sacred word is becoming vague or even disappearing. Do not worry; this is simply part of the process of Centering Prayer.

*4. At the end of the prayer period, remain in silence with eyes closed for two or three minutes.*

If this prayer is done in a group, the leader may slowly recite the "Our Father" during the additional two or three minutes while the others listen. The additional two or three minutes give the psyche time to readjust to the external senses and enable us to bring the atmosphere of silence into daily life.

It should be noted that the principal effects of Centering Prayer are experienced in daily life, not in the period of Centering Prayer itself.

The minimum time for this prayer is about twenty minutes. Two periods are recommended each day, one first thing in the morning, and one in the afternoon or early evening.

The end of the prayer period can be indicated by a timer, provided it does not have an audible tick or loud sound when it goes off.

Various physical irritations may be noticed during your prayer. These may include slight pains, itches, or twitches in various parts of the body, or a generalized restlessness. These are usually due to the untying of emotional knots in the body. You may also notice heaviness or lightness in the extremities. This is usually due to a deep level of spiritual attentiveness. In either case, pay no attention to them, or simply allow the mind to rest briefly in the sensation and then return to the sacred word.

Father Thomas Keating, O.C.S.O. (b. 1923), is a Cistercian monk and former abbot of St. Joseph's Abbey in Spencer, Massachusetts. He is the founder of Contemplative Outreach, the Snowmass Interreligious Conference, and a former president of the Temple of Understanding. The author of numerous books and articles on Christian contemplative practice, including *Open Mind, Open Heart, Manifesting God,* and *Divine Therapy & Addiction,* Father Keating is one of the foremost experts on the contemplative dimensions of Christian spirituality, and one of the most revered elders of the world's spiritual community. He currently resides at St. Benedict's Monastery in Snowmass, Colorado.

# THE BREATH WITHIN THE BREATH

## Yogi Nataraja Kallio

A STUDENT ONCE ASKED KABIR, one of India's most beloved poets and mystics, "Where is God to be found?" Kabir replied, "He is the breath within the breath." This famous utterance intimates how something as seemingly simple as the breath can be a doorway to connecting with Ultimate Reality.

In the Yoga tradition, breath practice is called *pranayama,* and is considered an essential tool not only for creating health and harmony in the body, but also for the expansion of consciousness and the realization of our true nature. The word, *pranayama* is comprised of two words: *prana,* 'life-force' or 'energy,' and *ayama,* 'expansion' or 'extension.' Though often thought of as a therapeutic practice, the deeper aim of pranayama is to purify, free and expand the energy of body and mind. For *pranayama* uses the physical breath to access and create change in the subtle breath or life-force.

According to Yoga philosophy, all experience is born of two fundamental principles: *prana,* 'life-force' and *chitta,* 'consciousness.' All that we experience—from the most manifest and dense to the most refined and subtle—is an expression of life-force, whereas that which experiences it is consciousness. Like two dancers moving in unison, these two principles are intimately related; a movement in one creates a reciprocal movement in the other. The *Hatha Yoga Pradipika* describes this relationship in the following way: "When *prana* moves, *chitta* moves. When *prana* is without movement, *chitta* is without movement." Thus, by moving our breath consciously, we can create an immediate shift in our state of mind.

Yoga practitioners believe that our subtle body is composed of numerous streams of life-force, called *nadis* in Sanskrit. Of these, the *sushumna nadi,* the 'hollow reed' is of greatest importance.

Situated along the central axis of the body, it is considered the central current of intelligence from which all the peripheral *nadis* radiate, and into which they absorb in moments of illumination. The *sushumna nadi,* which is also described as the 'staff of God,' the 'path of liberation,' and the 'pillar of light,' is the energetic correlate to non-dual awareness and the circuitry by which the divine force manifests in our life.

Indicating the importance of the *sushumna nadi* in Yogic practice, the culminating verse of the *Hatha Yoga Pradipika* states: "Until the *prana* has entered the *sushumna nadi* and the mind has assumed the form of *Brahman* (the Divine), all this talk of wisdom and knowledge is nothing but the nonsensical babbling of a madman."

From earth to heaven, the *sushumna nadi* can be sensed during moments of sincere prayer and aspiration as an ascending current of expansion. From heaven to earth, the *sushumna nadi* can be felt in moments of receptivity and surrender, as a current of grace, descending and integrating into one's being.

The ultimate intention of most *pranayama* practices, including the one described below, is to purify, awaken and unite the pranic force with the *sushumna nadi,* thereby impelling the peripheral or individual self to unite with the supreme Self.

## THE FULL YOGIC BREATH

The Full Yogic Breath is made up of four components, which, when practiced together, help us to unite mind and the life-force with the *sushumna nadi.*

### 1. Posture

The first component of the practice is posture. Like a mountain, whether seated on the ground or in a chair, the body must be upright, still and relaxed. This allows the spine of the physical body to be free from obstruction so that the subtle body can be felt without distraction.

Once seated in a fully upright and relaxed position, firmly root the sitting bones and slightly recoil the pelvic floor (perineum) towards the heart. This gesture is called *mulabandha* in Sanskrit and moves the pelvic force upwards towards the heart.[76]

## 2. Ujjayi Pranayama

The second component of the practice involves beginning to move the breath consciously through *ujjayi pranayama,* the 'upward moving, victorious breath.'

While breathing through the nose, slightly constrict the back of the throat (the glottis muscle), as if you were swallowing something. This narrows the passage through which the breath passes, which in turn lengthens the duration of the breath, as well as creating a soft, aspirate, whispering sound, similar to the sound of the ocean when heard from a distance.

This sound serves both as an anchor to focus the mind, as well as a mirror to reflect the relative smoothness, evenness and quality of the breath. For example, if the sound is loud at the beginning and soft or gasping at the end, it indicates that one is not breathing evenly. The aim is to breathe so that the sound is consistent from the inception to the end of the breath cycle.

## 3. Breathing the Entire Body

The third component of the practice involves lengthening the breath throughout the entire body, thereby mirroring the physical breath with the movement of the *sushumna nadi.*

The lungs can be divided into three sections: upper (upper torso and shoulders), middle (mid rib cage and heart), and lower (diaphragm to the middle ribs). The aim of the full Yogic breath is to breathe evenly through all three sections of the lungs.[77]

Though the physical breath is limited to the lungs, in this *pranayama,* the focus is on the sensation of the breath, which stretches through the entire body. During inhalation the breath stretches from the lower lungs, through the middle lungs, to the upper lungs, like a cup being filled with water; however, the sensation of the inhalation stretches all the way down to the base of the body, rooting in the pelvic floor, while simultaneously rising upwards towards the crown of the head.

With the exhalation, the 'cup' empties, as the breath releases from upper lungs to lower lungs; however the sensation of the breath descends (without collapsing the chest), all the way to the base of the torso.

To assist in this practice keep the lowest wall of the abdomen slightly lifted and toned. This allows the sensation of the breath to simultaneously descend all the way to the pelvic floor and rise towards the crown, without being consumed by the otherwise inflating belly.

THE FOUR FUNCTIONS OF THE BREATH

There are four aspects within a *pranayama* breath cycle: inhalation *(puraka)*, exhalation *(rechaka)*, retention after inhalation *(antar kumbhaka)*, and retention after exhalation *(bahir kumbhaka)*. Each serves a unique function in effecting change in the physical, subtle, and mental body.

INHALATION: "Inhalation *(puraka)* is the intake of cosmic energy by the individual for his growth and progress. . . . It is the Infinite uniting with the finite. It draws in the breath of life as carefully and as gently as the fragrance of a flower might be indrawn and distributes it evenly throughout the body."[78]

EXHALATION: "Exhalation is the outflow of the individual energy *(jivatma)* to unite with the cosmic energy *(Paramatma)*. It quietens [sic.] and silences the brain. It is the surrender of the sadhaka's ego to and immersion in the Self."[79]

RETENTION: As the breath is stilled, the prana is stilled, enabling the mind to become still as well. It is essential to know that this is the most powerful part of *pranayama* and must be treated extremely delicately. Never hold the breath to the point of creating any strain or tension.

Integrating all of the above points, a good introductory inhalation, exhalation, and retention ratio might be: 4-2-6-1.

1. Inhale for the count of 4, feeling the sensation of the inhalation, like a tree, simultaneously rooting through the base of the body as it ascends towards the crown;

2. Hold the breath in for the count of 2, being still, pausing at the end of the inhalation;

3. Exhale for the count of 6, feeling the sensation of the breath descend, while keeping the heart open, the body upright;

4. Hold the breath out for the count of 1, feeling the empty stillness;

5. This completes one round. Continue for 9-27 rounds.

As this ratio becomes comfortable, you can slightly increase the duration of each phase of the breath. At no point should there be any strain, as this will create a strain in the nervous system and mind. If you experience any tightness or strain, reduce the ratio of the breath and let the practice become more effortless.

### 4. Meditation on the Pillar of Light

The fourth and final component of the Full Yogic Breath involves the attunement of the mind with the subtle body. As the breath becomes more conscious and expansive, align your awareness with the *sushumna nadi* by feeling the sensations along the central axis of the body. Allow your awareness to unite with this innermost stream on sensation, feeling yourself as a pillar of light.

Finally, after completing a number of breath cycles, let the technique dissolve on the exhalation, and simply abide as awareness itself, the space in which life-force spontaneously unfolds. This is the essence of *pranayama,* the gateway to the breath within the breath.

The full possibility of what this practice intends may not be discovered immediately but requires regular practice. Initially the practice is to simply discover the subtleties involved in freeing the breath to flow evenly through the entire body. When the physical components of this practice become effortless, the attunement to the 'breath within the breath,' the *sushumna nadi,* becomes more accessible and spontaneous, allowing for its integration into all aspects of one's life.

Yogi Nataraja Kallio, M.A., is head of Yoga Teacher Training in the Traditional Eastern Arts program at Naropa University in Boulder, Colorado. Nataraja has been a student of Yoga for over twenty years, seven of which were spent studying in India. He has studied extensively in the lineages of Sri Aurobindo, Krishnamacharya (Iyengar, Ashtanga, and Viniyoga), Purna Yoga, Swami Sivananda, Swami Satyananda, Swami Gitananda, and the Tantric Sri Vidya tradition of South India. Nataraja has taught at Naropa University since 2000, and designed the Yoga Teacher Training concentration in 2006.

# THE ELEMENTAL PURIFICATION BREATHS

## Pir Zia Inayat-Khan

*Air, earth, water and fire are God's servants.*
*To us they seem lifeless, but to God living.*
— Jalal al-Din Rumi[80]

IN THE SIXTH CENTURY C.E. the Ka'ba at Mecca was an idol house where
an assortment of deities were routinely plied with fumigations and
sacrifices. But not all Meccans were votaries of the cult. Some were
convinced that the Ka'ba was the legacy of the prophet Abraham.
These loosely organized desert monotheists were known as *hanifs*.
Though lacking a bounded religious identity, the *hanifs* enjoyed
a fertile inner life. One of their practices was a form of meditative
retreat called *tahannuth*.

It was in the course of such a retreat, in a cave on Mount Hira,
that Muhammad (d. 632) received his first revelation. Borne by
the angel Gabriel, the revelation urged him, "Recite!" As the flow
of divine speech resumed, Muhammad recited to those who would
listen, beginning with his wife Khadija. Thus, over the space of two
decades, chapter-by-chapter the *Qur'an* descended to Earth.

In places, the Qur'an provides fascinating glimpses into
Muhammad's personal mystical experiences. The ninety-fourth
chapter *(al-Inshirah,* 'The Opening Up') describes how the
Prophet's breast was opened and his heart purified. Other verses
(17:1, 53:7-18) speak of a "night journey" to Jerusalem, whereupon
the Prophet ascended the empyrean and approached the presence
of the God.

Among Muhammad's followers were a cadre of disciples who
sought to emulate him not merely exoterically but also esoterically,
undertaking a regimen of interior purification and uninterrupted
remembrance of God (invoked in Arabic as *Allah).*[81] In time these
initiates and their heirs became known as Sufis.

Early definitions of Sufism *(tasawwuf)* highlight the moral and spiritual disposition of its practitioners. The Sufi was one who "possesses nothing and is possessed by nothing," who "sees nothing but God in the two worlds," whose "thought keeps pace with his foot," and whose "language, when he speaks, is the reality of his state." For some, the very act of naming Sufism was inimical. One Sufi lamented, "Sufism was a reality without a name that has become a name without a reality."[82]

Such scruples notwithstanding, between the tenth and thirteenth centuries Sufism transformed itself into a large-scale social, intellectual and spiritual movement driven by organized mystical orders spread across the Afro-Eurasian *oikumene*, from Andalusia to Hindustan. Common to all of these groups was the project of seeking nearness with God through individual and collective spiritual practice. Within this shared framework, each order developed a method of practice more or less unique to itself.

In South Asia, the Chishti Order attained special prominence. Brought to India by Mu'in al-Din Chishti (d. 1236) and Qutb al-Din Bakhtiyar Kaki (d. 1235), it rapidly grew in influence under their successors, Farid al-Din Ganj-i Shakar (d. 1265), Nizam al-Din Awliya' (d. 1325), and Nasir al-Din Chiragh (d. 1351). All of these adepts taught silent, heart-centered contemplation *(muraqaba)* as a core practice. Nizam al-Din Awliya' attributed his method of contemplation to Abu Bakr al-Shibli (d. 945), who learned it by watching a cat poised motionless before a mouse hole.[83]

In the Mughal era, Shah Kalim Allah Jahanabadi (d. 1729) compiled a systematic exposition of the major practices of the Chishti Order entitled *Kashkul-i Kalimi*. Shah Kalim Allah positions contemplation as the first stage in a three-fold process. At the stage of contemplation the seeker looks with closed eyes into the heart and visualizes God's presence within it. Later, at the stage of meditation *(mushahada),* the seeker looks toward the sky and imagines leaving the body and approaching God through the celestial spheres. Finally, at the stage of beholding *(mu'ayana),* the seeker's heart is permanently anchored in the seventh heaven by means of a golden thread.[84]

In the early twentieth century, the Chishti-Nizami-Kalimi branch of the Sufi tree flowered in the life and teachings of Inayat Khan (d. 1927). Enjoined by his teacher to bring Sufism to the West, Inayat Khan traveled extensively in the United States and Europe and in

1917 officially established his Sufi Order in London. Building on the work of his Chishti predecessors, he developed a curriculum of esoteric study emphasizing four phases of spiritual practice: concentration, contemplation, meditation, and realization. Moving through these grades, the practitioner progressively learns to focus attention, refine thought, transcend thought in pure luminous awareness, and ultimately to integrate transcendent and immanent modes of cognition.

The roots of Inayat Khan's methodology were not only Islamic, but also Indic. His transmission connected, as he phrased it, "two lines of the prophetic mission, the Hindu line and that of Beni Israel."[85] The Mughal crown prince Dara Shikuh characterized the encounter between the wisdom of the Qur'an and that of the Upanishads as a "merging of two oceans."[86] More than any other order, the Chishtis actively fostered this cultural and spiritual exchange.

Sufism and Yoga are distinctly different systems of knowledge and practice. They are united, however, by their mutual possession of an elementalist cosmology.[87] In both traditions, the elements are reverenced as primal sacred forces. For the Sufis, the elements are four in number: earth, water, fire and air. In addition to these the Vedic worldview posits a fifth element or *quintessence:* ether *(akash).*

Sufism and Yoga concur that, at the level of latent perfection, the human being is a microcosm of the universe *('alam saghir),* physically, psychologically and spiritually endowed with the pure qualities of the four elements. For this potential to be actualized, the human form must be realigned with its cosmic matrix, the animate Earth. To accomplish this, Sufis and Yogis practice a shared repertory of exercises that function to harmonize the elements within and without.

The practice that follows is a notable exercise of this kind. Transmitted by Inayat Khan, it serves as a foundational practice within the Order he founded. While most of the esoteric disciplines taught in the Order are reserved for initiates, this simple yet profound practice is an open one. Ideally it is to be done early in the morning, outside or before an open window.

THE PRACTICE

Sit or stand in silence, erect but relaxed. Close your eyes.

### Earth

Inhale and exhale through the nose five times. Stimulate the horizontal motion of the subtle energetic current of the breath. Attune to the color yellow. Identify with stone, sand, loam, and clay. Feel the bone, gristle, flesh and skin of which your body is made. Sense the chthonic dimension of your psyche, the qualities of stability, patience and humility.

### Water

Inhale through the nose and exhale through the mouth five times. Stimulate the descending motion of the subtle energetic current of the breath. Attune to the color green. Identify with waves, whirlpools, torrents and rivulets. Feel the blood and lymph flowing within you, answering the beat of your heart. Sense the aqueous dimension of your psyche, the qualities of purity, compassion and generosity.

### Fire

Inhale through the mouth and exhale through the nose five times. Stimulate the ascending motion of the subtle energetic current of the breath. Attune to the color red. Identify with lava, flame, sparks, and light. Feel the metabolic heat radiating from your body. Sense the igneous dimension of your psyche, the qualities of ardor and burning conviction.

### Air

Inhale through the mouth and exhale through the mouth five times. Stimulate the chaotic, zigzag motion of the subtle energetic current of the breath. Attune to the color blue. Identify with the sky, the breeze, clouds, and bubbles. Feel the oxygen whirling in the airways of your body. Sense the aerial dimension of your psyche, the qualities of buoyancy, freedom, and elation.

Pause to notice the harmony of the four elements within you. Open your eyes, and conclude with the following prayer (*Nayaz*):

*Beloved Lord, Almighty God!*
*Through the rays of the sun,*
*Through the waves of the air,*
*Through the All-pervading Life in space,*
*Purify and revivify me, and, I pray,*
*Heal my body, heart, and soul.*
*Amen.*

Pir Zia Inayat-Khan is the son and successor of Pir Vilayat Inayat-Khan and president of the Sufi Order International. In addition to the interfaith mystical training he has received from his father, Pir Zia has studied Buddhism under the auspices of His Holiness, the Dalai Lama, and Sufism in the classical Indian tradition of the Chishtiyya. Pir Zia is the author of *Saracen Chivalry: Counsels on Valor, Generosity and the Mystical Quest* (2012), and editor of *Caravan of Souls: An Introduction to the Sufi Path of Hazrat Inayat Khan* (2013). He holds a doctorate in Religion from Duke University.

# BREATHING THE DIVINE NAME

## Rabbi Jeff Roth

FOR THIS PRACTICE, we will make an explicit link to the most holy name for God in the Jewish tradition, *Yud Hay Vav Hay,* also called the *tetragrammaton.* These syllables are the names of the four Hebrew letters that comprise this most holy name, *Y-H-V-H.* The letter yud has the sound of the English letter *y.* The letter *hay* corresponds to the English *h.* The letter vav is like the letter *v* in English. The Jewish mystical tradition gives us a framework for understanding these four letters of God's name. Let's begin with the letter *hay,* or *h.* As you may have noticed, this letter appears twice in this name for God. If you intone the letter out loud, you will immediately recognize that it is the sound of breathing. Try this: breathe out loudly enough for an extended time so that you can hear the sound of the breath with your own ears. Now, if you do the same thing when inhaling, you'll hear that the in-breath also makes the same sound. The perspective that pronouncing the letter *hay* is the same sound as breathing makes an explicit link between the breath and God's name.

It may not come as a surprise that God's name is connected to the breath. Most religious traditions connect breath with life and with God. The English word *spirit* is related to the word *respiration.* In Hebrew, the words for 'soul' *(neshamah)* and 'breath' *(nesheemah)* have the same root. *Ruah* means 'spirit' in Hebrew, but it is also a word for the wind, or movement of air, which is like the breath. In Genesis 2:7, when God wanted to make human beings, God breathed into the dust of the earth: "And *Y-H-V-H,* God, formed the human, of the dust from the soil, he blew into his nostrils the breath of life and the human became a living being." So when we pay attention to the breath, it is a way of paying attention to the divine animating life-force, which is inherent in each breath while we are still alive.

We have looked at two of the letters (the second and fourth) in the divine name, *hay* and *hay*. The other letters of the divine name provide different insights into the nature of God. The first letter is the *yud*. In Hebrew, this is the smallest letter of the alphabet and when written, its essence is the same as a single point. Since a point has no dimensions in time and space (its scientific definition), we need to draw something bigger than a point so that it can be seen. But Jewish mystics have always understood that the *yud* is connected to the concept of nothingness or emptiness. If we make a link to the breath, as we did for the letter *hay*, then we might consider that the *yud* in God's name corresponds to the state of emptiness that occurs before the in-breath begins. At that point, as the lungs have emptied of air, they contract, like a deflating balloon. While they do not disappear into nothingness, they do get to be their smallest size. Similarly, *yud* does not disappear, but is the smallest letter. If *yud* represents the empty place before the start of the in-breath, then the first *hay* in the divine name corresponds to the in-breath itself.

At the end of the in-breath, before the start of the out-breath, the lungs are now in their most expanded state. This can be called the full state. This full state can be linked to the Hebrew letter *vav*. *Vav* is the straightest letter in the Hebrew alphabet, written as simply a single straight line. To again use the image of a balloon, picture the long, skinny balloons used by people who make balloon animals. Before you start blowing it up, it hangs down, out of your mouth. As you blow it up, it straightens into a single straight line. In this way, vav can be thought of as fullness. Just as the lungs are full at the end of the in-breath.

We can now see that the whole cycle of breathing is coded within the divine name *Yud Hay Vav Hay,* as follows:

*Yud*—Empty

*Hay*—In

*Vav*—Full

*Hay*—Out

### BREATHING AND THE DIVINE PRESENCE

To begin the practice of concentrating on your breath, sit comfortably in a quiet place where you won't be disturbed. Turn off the ringer of your phone. You might begin this and any formal practice session by making the following intention: the act I am about to perform, I do for the sake of waking up to the Divine Presence that pervades all life, in order that I might become an aide in helping all beings to awaken and live in peace and joy.

As you begin to sit quietly, start by noticing whatever thoughts or feelings are present in your mind before you pointedly direct your attention anywhere. After a few moments of this, begin to focus your attention on the arising and passing of each breath. Allow the breath to come and go at its own pace. Don't try to manipulate the breath in any way. See if you can make the primary object of focus the physical sensations that accompany the breath. At the same time, softly begin to connect in your mind the four parts of the breath to the four letters of God's name. When you feel the bodily sensations that are present after the emptying of air from your lungs, silently say to yourself, *"Yud."* As you notice the in-breath arising and the accompanying bodily sensations, say to yourself, *"Hay."* You might extend the inner noting of the word *hay* to cover the whole period of the in-breath. When the in-breath finishes, try to feel the sensations in your body that are present before the out-breath begins, and say to yourself, *"Vav."* As the out-breath begins, say to yourself, *"Hay,"* and extend that noting as long as the out-breath is occurring. Continue to feel the physical sensations in your body as you breathe out.

Repeat this pattern of connecting the letters of the divine name to the parts of your breath for ten minutes. While we begin with the intention to aim and sustain the attention on the object of focus, it is inevitable that your mind will wander. Try not to worry about it or judge yourself. Judging yourself discourages you from practicing because you feel "You're not good at it." It doesn't mean you are a bad meditator; it is just the nature of our minds to be distracted. When you find your attention wandering, simply bring your focus back to your breath and the connection to the divine name. This returning of the attention back to the object of focus is central to concentration practice.

You only need to cultivate the practice of noticing as soon as possible when your attention has wandered. And when you notice that, make a decision to return. This is a skill that can be developed over time. Eventually, you will notice that your ability to sustain your attention on the object of focus will grow. But don't expect your progress to be overly linear in development. Some days your ability to sustain your attention will be better than others. This may be true over periods of weeks or months as well, depending on many other factors that affect your life. For example, you might be less able to sustain your attention during times of life stress than in calm times.

You may find that you continue to judge yourself when your attention wanders. If so, you can work with this in your meditation. When you notice self-criticism, simply file this awareness away for future exploration. This is an example of concentration and awareness coming together. Negative self-judgment is one of the biggest impediments to waking up. For one thing, it makes us feel badly about ourselves, which is not very helpful when it comes to staying in the present moment. Ultimately, cultivating an attitude of self-acceptance is a crucial component of the growth that occurs as you see clearly the challenges you face in trying to be more awake in your life. Indeed, self-acceptance is a precursor to the deep happiness that is possible through this practice.

You might want to undertake this practice daily while working with this book, especially, if you just beginning to explore meditation. But it may be that using the names of the Hebrew letters *yud, hay, vav,* and *hay* is too abstract for you. In that case, consider using the words *empty, in, full,* and *out* instead. English words may resonate for some people more than the Hebrew letters. You might try the practice each way and see which words better help you sustain your attention to the breath.*

Rabbi Jeff Roth is one of the primary teachers of The Awakened Heart Project for Contemplative Judaism, promoting the use of Jewish contemplative techniques that foster the development of a heart of wisdom and compassion. He was also the co-founder of Elat Chayyim Jewish Renewal Retreat Center, which he served as Executive Director and Spiritual Director for 13 years. He is an experienced meditation teacher, a facilitator of Jewish retreats, and the author of *Jewish Meditation Practices for Everyday Life: Awakening Your Heart, Connecting with God* (2009). For more information on the Awakened Heart Project, see www.awakenedheartproject.org.

# THE BREATH OF TAO

## Kenneth Cohen

OF THE THREE great teachings *(san jiao)* of ancient China—Confucianism, Buddhism, and Taoism—only Taoism may be called an indigenous Chinese religion. Confucianism is a philosophy that emphasizes ethics and social harmony. Buddhism searches for the cause of suffering through meditation and introspection. It is an import from India and had to adapt to pre-existing Taoist philosophy and monastic customs. But Taoism is essentially Chinese, a combination of even earlier shamanism, called *wu jiao* in Chinese, and spiritual practices established by mountain hermits. These hermits were drawn to the beauty, power, and peace of nature. Some were former government employees who escaped from the chaos, intrigue, and aggression common during the early centuries B.C.E.. If they were successful in their quest for a deeper truth, they merged with the spirit of the nature, achieved health and longevity, and became the realized sages that in Taoism are known as 'Immortals' *(Xian)*.

Why is this tradition called Taoism? It is based on the Tao, literally a 'road' or 'trail.' The Tao is the path of nature and naturalness. The goal of Taoism is summarized in the opening line of the *Tao Te Ching* (Classic of the Tao and Its Virtue), written by the philosopher Lao Tzu in the fourth century B.C., "The Tao that can be spoken of is not the Tao." Why can't you speak about the Tao, the Way of Nature? Because you are it! There is no outside perspective. Humans may think and act as though they are separate from nature, and thus have the right to manipulate it without consequence, but is this really true? Are we supernatural or even unnatural? I don't think so. You can no more talk objectively about the Tao than you can use a sword to cut itself or lift yourself up by your own bootstraps. The Tao is where words begin: subject undivided from object. What is that which produces thoughts, what is that state of silent being from which words arise?

To answer this question is a logical impossibility.

Additionally, because life, the Tao, is always changing, how can words, which require fixed definitions, ever represent it? If you can capture the wind or flowing water in a bucket, then you can describe the Tao! The Tao that can be described is not the Tao, because the mystery of nature must be experienced. It flows and changes from moment to moment.

Thus, observation and meditation are central to understanding Taoism. Taoist monasteries are *guan,* "observatories," places to observe nature and one's inner nature. To observe accurately requires freeing the mind of preconceptions, prejudices, and cultural filters. A Taoist must cease being a Taoist; he or she must *un-know.* "The scholar seeks to gain day by day, "writes Lao Tzu, "the Taoist seeks to lose day by day. Losing and losing until reaching the effortless state where nothing happens *(wu wei)!"* The mind returns to its roots. Lao Tzu continues, "Use the outer light to return to insight." Complexity returns to simplicity. Existence itself merges with the great emptiness where no division exists. This is not the emptiness of nihilism, as though the world loses its meaning. Just the contrary—emptiness is the freedom of space, where there are no ruts to follow and all possibilities exist. It is a kind of mental suppleness.

We find a beautiful summary of these ideas and of the essence of Taoist meditation in chapter 40 of the *Tao Te Ching:*

> *Reversal is the movement of the Tao;*
> *Suppleness is the function of the Tao.*
> *Under heaven, all things are born of being;*
> *And being is born of Emptiness.*[88]

There are many forms of Taoist meditation, including visualizations to realize the unity of microcosm and macrocosm; *qigong* (life-energy) meditations to clear the acupuncture meridians of obstructions; methods of absorbing life-force from the sun, moon, and stars; and internal alchemy to combine the interior subtle energies and create the "golden elixir" of health and wisdom. In this chapter, I will teach you two of the most classic and revered Taoist meditations, called "embryonic respiration" and "whole body breathing." The goal is learn to breathe innocently and deeply like a newborn baby. Breath is a reminder that life is not a possession. We allow nature as air into the body; we let it go. Breathing teaches us to surrender to the wisdom of the Tao as manifest in our body's natural rhythms. In chapter 10 of the *Tao Te Ching,* Lao Tzu says:

> *Controlling the yang and yin, embracing the One.*
> *Can you not allow separation?*
> *Concentrating the qi, attaining suppleness,*
> *Can you become like a child?*

EMBRYONIC RESPIRATION

Find a time in the morning or evening when you will not be disturbed. Sit on a cushion on the floor or on a chair. Wear comfortable clothes. Loosen your belt if you need to. The back is straight but not stiff. Your lower body feels rooted into the ground, and your head is lifted slightly towards the sky. You are relaxed, using minimal effort to maintain an elegant posture. To encourage healthy breathing, it is especially important to release the chest and the abdomen. Neither lift nor depress the breastbone. The lower abdomen, between the navel and pubic bone, is free of tension and fully capable of moving as you breathe. This may take patience and practice, as many people unconsciously hold the belly in or try to make it appear flat. This interferes with breathing and makes one energy-starved. Once you have learned these various techniques and no longer need to follow the instructions, try the meditations with the eyes lightly closed. Lower the eyelids as though gently lowering a curtain.

### Stage 1: Deep Breathing: Shen Hu Xi

Breathe slowly, silently, and naturally. When you inhale through the nose, the belly gently expands. When you exhale through the mouth, it releases, effortlessly. With each inhalation imagine that you are drawing-in the pure energy of the universe. It spreads through your entire body, refreshing and renewing you. With each exhalation, you release the old, unneeded energy. Do this for ten breaths, silently counting your exhalations.

### Stage 2: Gathering Life-Force: Cai Qi Fa

From this stage onwards, all of your breathing, inhalation and exhalation, is through the nose (unless you have a nasal or sinus obstruction, in which case adjust as needed). Continue with abdominal breathing, inhaling the belly expands; exhaling it lets go. Remember, don't exert force, trust nature to move your breath without your help!

As you inhale, imagine breath energy goes to the center of the chest near the breastbone, as though you have a small energy reservoir there. As you exhale, imagine the breath drops down from the chest to the lower abdomen, to a reservoir about 1.5 inches below the navel and about three inches inwards (in the direction of the lower back). This lower reservoir is called the *dan tian,* 'the elixir field.' Practice ten repetitions. Every inhalation brings *qi* to the chest; every exhalation drops the *qi* into its storage tank, the abdominal *dan tian.*

### *Stage 3: Internal Breathing:* Nei Hu Xi

Continuing with silent abdominal respiration, in and out through the nose, as you inhale imagine that the breath is an internal current of *qi* (life-force) that rises from the *dan tian* to the chest. As you exhale, the breath drops from the chest back down to the *dan tian.* Thus, although you are, of course, continuing to breathe naturally, in your mind the breath is entirely an internal current of energy. Inhaling, breath rises from abdomen to chest. Exhaling, breath descends from chest to abdomen. Up and down, up and down, ten repetitions. This method is sometimes called "the mixing of fire (heart) and water (kidneys)."

### *Stage 4: Effortless Breathing:* Wu Wei Hu Xi

Continuing, now keep your mind on the gentle opening and closing of the abdomen as you inhale and exhale. When you inhale, don't suck the breath in. When you exhale, don't push the breath out. Discover the natural pace of your breath. Get out of the way and don't interfere. Can you be aware of the four stages of breathing: 1. the way breath comes in; 2. the turning of the breath between inhale and exhale; 3. the exhalation; and 4. the natural pause that occurs at the end of the exhale before breath comes back in?

Pay attention to these stages for a few minutes. The points of the turning of the breath between inhale and exhale and again between exhale and inhale are between *yin* and *yang*. They are gateways to stillness. If you allow all four stages, never deliberately sucking, pushing, or holding the breath, your breathing rate will slow down. Practice for about five to ten minutes. This stage flows naturally into the next.

### *Stage 5: Embryonic Respiration:* Tai Xi

Now the breath seems to neither rise nor fall, neither open nor close. It is so ultra-slow and soft that if a down feather were held in front of the nostrils, it wouldn't move. Your mind merges with the breath, as though the breath is your entire world. The belly is pleasantly warm. You are like a mother nurturing her womb with caring, compassionate awareness. You are breathing like a baby in the womb of creation. Enjoy as long as you wish (or if you must look at a clock, I suggest twenty to thirty minutes).

### *Whole Body Breathing:* Zheng Ti Hu Xi

Follow the same 'Basics' described at the beginning of Embryonic Respiration. Now imagine that the body is so open, so light, so receptive, that every cell is breathing (which, scientifically speaking, is true). With each gentle inhalation, your whole body is refreshed. Fresh *qi* goes to the skin, the muscles and tendons, the nerves, the internal organs, the joints, the bones. There is no place that can resist the breath. And with every effortless exhalation, every tissue and cell lets go of what it no longer needs. The breath is a gentle breeze, and every part of your body is a sail that can respond to it. Taoists say that a sage can breathe with the feet. Can you breathe with your feet, with your ears, your fingers, the crown of your head? What do you need to adjust so that your whole body is breathing? Practice for ten to fifteen minutes or for whatever period feels comfortable.

## Closing & Opening Words

Breath is life. Breath is Tao. We can survive for a long time without food or water; but deprived of the invisible air, we count our lives in minutes. No wonder all of the world's religions acknowledge its importance. It is *qi* in Taoism, *prana* in Hinduism, *ruah* and *ruh* to Jews and Muslims, *pneuma* to the Christians, and acknowledged with a myriad of other names by the indigenous peoples of Africa, Australia, and the Americas. If only the world's religious leaders would remember that we all breathe the same air, the pathway to peace would be obvious.


Kenneth Cohen (Gao Han) is a well-known Qigong Master and Taoist scholar/initiate. He was a student and friend of Alan Watts and former apprentice to Taoist Abbott Huang Gengshi. Ken is the author of *The Way of Qigong: The Art and Science of Chinese Energy Healing* (Ballantine Books), *Taoism: Essential Teachings of the Way and Its Power* (Sounds True audio), and more than 200 articles on spirituality and health. He is the founder and director of the Qigong Research and Practice Center (www.qigonghealing.com).

# Appendix A

## Via Positiva and Via Negativa:
### Two Complimentary Approaches
### to Meditation

GENERALLY SPEAKING, we come to know things through both positive and negative mental processes. For example, when our eyes focus on a tall woody pillar growing out of the ground with branches and leaves, our mind quickly processes this information and assigns the category 'tree' to this thing we are looking at. This process of deduction is a positive process. However, our mind can also determine that this thing is a 'tree' by eliminating all other possibilities. For instance, by noticing that it is not like a rock, a plant, a bush, or anything else. This process of elimination is a negative process, accomplished by negation.

When it comes to achieving the goals of spiritual practice, we simultaneously attempt to accumulate virtues, such as compassion and wisdom, while eliminating the vices, ignorance and negative emotions that are the obstacles to these virtuous states of mind. We try to accumulate wisdom and eliminate ignorance, to accumulate generosity and eliminate selfishness, and so forth—adding and subtracting, continually applying both a positive and a negative approach to our spiritual practice.

In cultivating a healthy mind through the techniques of meditation and contemplation, it is also helpful to utilize both 'positive' and 'negative' processes. These process are not positive and negative in these sense of 'good' and 'bad,' of course, but rather in the way we might speak of 'positive and negative space' when looking at art. Positive and negative processes in meditation are often determined by their varying levels of concern with a meditative 'object' or 'sacred attributes,' or by how they either construct or deconstruct a view of reality. For instance, a negative process might aim at eliminating ignorance and the faulty mental 'programs' that cause us unhappiness. A positive process, on the other hand, might aim at replacing these faulty programs with those that create happiness. At first, this may seem simplistic; but on closer inspection, the strategic deployment of both negative and positive methods is quite profound and can yield dramatic results.

In spiritual terminology, the 'negative' approach is often called the *via negativa,* or 'negative way,' because it clears away the obstacles to a properly functioning, pure and happy mind. Once again, in the language of computer technology, the negative approach can help us to 'debug' or eliminate the 'faulty code' of a program that causes it to malfunction. The term used for this approach to meditation or theology in Christian circles is apophatic, from the Greek, *apophanai,* 'to say no.'[89] In Buddhist and Hindu traditions, this negative approach stems from the Sanskrit *apoha,* which implies a way of knowing an object through eliminating everything that this object *is not.* With regard to meditation, this can be compared to a process of *kenosis,*[90] of self-emptying, opening up and clearing out, breaking the hold of the 'false self' and allowing the ego to merge with God or the Ultimate Reality.

For example, the Hesychast tradition of Eastern Orthodox Christianity applies the *via negativa* principle in their meditations of the heart. When they are in the ecstasy of approaching unity, or conceptualizing God, Hesychast contemplatives quell these distractions by meditating on the *no-thing-ness* of God, since the Divine should not be imprisoned in limitations of our mind and body. For in both our blissful experiences and in our concepts we are setting limits upon the Divine which are really based on our own limited capacities. Therefore, apophatic meditation deepens the unity with the Divine by emptying out the limitations of human perception and sensation.

In Buddhist terminology, the *via negativa* is cultivated through meditations on Emptiness, which is the English translation for the Sanskrit term, *shunyata.* In the Buddhist context, Emptiness is the absolute truth of existence, but it can also connote a process of emptying oneself of false projections about the nature of conventional reality.[91]

Although there are important differences between the Christian and Buddhist concepts of 'emptying,' both systems seem to support the idea that a consciousness emptied of false notions of being can make way for a pure state of awareness that is by nature, tranquil, compassionate, and free from suffering. This un-afflicted state of clear consciousness yields a sublime, non-dual wisdom, and a unity between the individual 'self' or 'soul' and the universally true state of existence. While there might be disagreement about the name and definition of this universal truth, it seems that the process for perceiving it, or opening into it, has much in common.

The process of InterSpiritual Meditation makes room for a wide variety of meditative approaches, and even 'truths.' It does so by providing a format and process within which each meditator has the freedom of his or her own practice and beliefs. Even as each of us individually rely on the metaphysics and methods of our specific spiritual traditions, this InterSpiritual Meditation process helps us to comprehend the deep contemplative processes shared by our various traditions. In this case, the notion of becoming 'empty,' i.e., emptying ourselves of limited preconceptions and false projections, helps us to open our consciousness to a direct perception and (depending on our tradition) a non-dual knowingness of that which we regard as the Absolute Truth.

The correlative approach to the *via negativa* is the *via positiva,* or 'positive way,' which replaces the 'faulty code' or knowledge with a 'good code,' allowing our consciousness to be happy, healthy, and in harmony with sacred dimensions of being. The Christian term for this is cataphatic, from the Greek, *cataphasis,* meaning 'to affirm' or 'to speak about.'[92] Cataphatic approaches cover all of the positive attributes of spirituality and spiritual practice: these include the attributes of love, compassion, kindness, wisdom, and faith, cultivated by contemplation, devotional prayer, ritual, and service to others.

While many positive qualities can be accumulated through our proactive thoughts, words, and actions, they may not fully infuse our entire being unless we simultaneously empty ourselves through the apophatic processes. This is why many of the world's great religions contain both positive and negative methods for purifying our consciousness. In my own experience, I have found that spiritual practice often requires a combination of both positive and negative approaches. In a sense, they are interdependent, and their metaphysical and practical implications become more and more refined and subtle as our spiritual practice matures and begins to bear fruit.

# APPENDIX B

## WAY-POINTS ON THE CONTEMPLATIVE JOURNEY

OVER THE YEARS, experience has taught me that there are many temporary 'way-points' of realization along the contemplative journey. If we are not careful, we can easily mistake any number of these way-points for some kind of end-point, discovering, somewhere down the line, that our attachment to it has inflated us with false, self-destructive pride. Like many artists and athletes, we learn that our personal best cannot be known without years of training, perseverance, and revised expectations. Thus, new way-points emerge as reflections of our spiritual maturity.

In my mid-twenties, when my passion for the spiritual life first blossomed, I was buoyed by a newly re-defined sense of manhood, and I quickly set about trying to live up to it with great zeal, taking pride in giving up the pleasures of the body, cultivating compassion, silence, non-violence, and meditation. The archetypal image of the 'spiritual warrior' I cultivated in my youth arose out of the writings of Martin Luther King Jr. and my work with black civil rights leaders. I was also inspired by the examples of Mahatma Gandhi and the Dalai Lama. This new vision of 'spiritual manhood' energized me through my doctoral studies as well as my life in Tibetan Buddhist monasteries. My intellectual confidence gave rise to an abiding faith that I was truly on the 'right path.'

But while this sense of 'spiritual warriorship' was an important ally early on in my spiritual journey, it wasn't sufficient to bring me tranquility and meaning in times of emotional hardship and illness. It took many more years before I began to glimpse the necessary inevitability of self-surrender, and a time when I would have to jettison the spiritual warrior stage of spiritual development. The painful transition I went through was a direct consequence of my early spiritual pride.

Surrender only began after nearly thirty years of practice. After pursuing a professional life based on will-power, cleverness, and personal persuasion; after doing my best as a community activist to do some good in the world; after years of balancing my Buddhist practice with an active life; after several bouts with pneumonia and two near-death-experiences—it finally happened. When I had reached a point in my meditation where 'manly effort' was no longer efficacious or useful, I was asked to simply rest, to meld, to receive, and to give up the effort that had led my to this point. I discovered that there is a point in one's practice when many techniques have been learned, the garden of the mind has been cultivated, the sails have been set to receive the mystic winds, our cocoon for transformation has been spun, and we must simply, patiently, receptively *abide in silence.*

We simply sit in internal silence, experiencing the individual boundaries of consciousness dissolving, emptying their self-identity, continually being infused by a vibrant clarity, a lightness of being, an intuition of the whole and all its interdependent parts, evaporating into the loving, forgiving, intuitively direct perception of the heart.

These moments of stillness are not passive, for they are built on years of training and practice. They don't entail simply waiting for something to happen. The sharpness of mind is not dulled by surrender and the process of transformation does not cease. And yet, the ongoing process is effortless and not restrained by impatience, desire, or our outmoded afflicted emotions. Unfettered, our consciousness is absorbed in its ultimate purpose—resting gently just beyond the veil—bathed in the mystery of being. This way-point might be called 'absorption in the nameless.'

With surrender comes a fearless absorption into the ineffable mystery of that which lies beyond the conceptual way-points of our life-long spiritual journeys. Gradually, the attributes of this absorption infuse our daily lives with words of wisdom, deeds of kind and compassionate service, and thoughts of courageous commitment and gentleness of being.

*Resting here,*
*Another waypoint emerges on the horizon;*
*A sweet scent carried on gentle breath;*
*As esoteric seeds planted years ago begin to ripen.*

# APPENDIX C

## WORKING WITH IMAGINATION & BLISS

IMAGINATION IS ONE of the more powerful contemplative tools we have at our disposal, for mental images are continually conditioning our bodies, minds, relationships, and physical environments. Imagination is a natural capacity of the human being and we are constantly creating and receiving spontaneous images through which we form our reality. Therefore, these internal projections become the lenses through which we perceive and interpret our private view of reality, and govern the future shape and health of our mind and body.

Imaginal meditations turn this ordinary human activity into an intentional process of carefully discerning and determining the specific images we would like to create and project. Highly sophisticated imaginal practices can be found in the Buddhist and Hindu Tantras where they enable practitioners to actualize the virtuous qualities of deities and actually transform themselves into the body and mind of a divine or sacred being. But there are also a wide variety of ancient and modern imaginal techniques that are slightly less ambitious in their goals. They simply facilitate the actualization of mental calm, healing, self-confidence, shaping the inner and outer environments for our future state of being.

As with other forms of meditation, it is important to discern the suitability of a specific imaginal meditation for us, and to consult with authentic teachers who can help us determine the approaches that best suit our experience, capacity, and expectations.

### WORKING WITH BLISS

It is no secret that meditation can make us feel really good inside. Some meditators might also experience states of extreme bliss and even euphoria. Among an InterSpiritual group of meditators, it is quite possible that experienced practitioners from different traditions will be experiencing various grades of bliss simultaneously. Yet the causes of this bliss might be explained differently by different traditions. Some might feel that bliss is the result of a certain breathing technique. Others might say that it is the awakening of *kundalini* energy, or a non-dual experience of the Divine.

As far as I know, neurological science has not devised a test to measure and compare 'bliss states' arising from different types of meditation. So it is not yet possible to assign specific bliss states to specific meditational stimuli. Nor is it possible to assign a grade to bliss states in such a way to say, for instance, that a meditation on Emptiness produces better bliss than meditation on Nature!

Among experienced meditators, open discussions of euphoria and bliss are rare and not encouraged, except perhaps with a qualified teacher. 'Bliss talk' has the danger of amplifying ego and mistaking the value of bliss with the actual purpose of meditation. While bliss is enthralling, it isn't generally considered a spiritual goal, nor is it proof of having achieved the goal. It can be the result of a meditation session, but not its purpose. In fact, it can be a giant distraction. Like sexual orgasm, it can create unhealthy attachment, and even an addiction. Those who experience euphoria might fall prey to cultivating techniques that produce it rather than attending to more sublime purposes whose intent might be unity with ultimate truth and compassionate service of others.

Euphoria can be produced by drugs, hyperventilation, and even prolonged and concentrated physical exercise: runners, cyclists, and swimmers all report endorphin-stimulated highs that result from single-focused, steady-breathing activity; lovers routinely experience the bliss of orgasm. None of these claim a spiritual cause for their bliss.

Nevertheless, there are also certain meditative techniques that are carefully employed during simulated or actual moments of sexual orgasm, as well as meditations designed for the moment of death, when consciousness is said to be absorbed in clear light and unimpeded euphoric states. It is during these moments that highly developed meditators might be able to accentuate spiritual absorption in the Divine in a way that may not possible during ordinary states of consciousness, possibly allowing for dramatic shifts in consciousness and accelerated spiritual progress.

While these practices are often romanticized by spiritual neophytes (and clever entrepreneurs in the spiritual marketplace), they should only be undertaken with proper training and great caution by advanced practitioners. For it is very easy to fall prey to the bliss-longing while maintaining the pretence of spiritual intent. This form of narcissism precipitates a fall into emotional difficulties, loss of reputation, and other serious setbacks to spiritual progress. In all religions we can find accounts of spiritual teachers who misused the devotion of others for sexual gratification or material gain in the guise of spiritual enlightenment.

In my own experience, and in my conversations with mature teachers and practitioners, I have learned how very experienced meditators can utilize meditative bliss as a vehicle to even more profound states of consciousness. Here, euphoria becomes the object for self-emptying, for de-reifying, for dissolving into even more sublime states of tranquility, equanimity and absorption that qualitatively transcend those preliminary states of euphoric bliss. Once euphoria and bliss are themselves transformed, there are no worldly temptations left to impede the eternal peace, wisdom, and compassion of authentic contemplative and meditative practice.

Then, we can walk through the day and dream through the night simultaneously observing, participating and maintaining a steady state of equanimity, wisdom and compassion.

*Empathetic, liberated and enlightened*
*We are lovingly engaged.*
*Healing the suffering of this world.*

# APPENDIX D

# InterSpiritual Meditation Verses

## I. May We be Happy and Healthy

In all the world
I cannot find
The source of peace
Outside my mind.

Neither play, nor drink,
Nor sex, nor food,
Can cause a constant
Blissful mood.

The things I see,
Touch, smell, taste, hear,
Cause both joy and pain,
Hope and fear.

Meditation relieves
my mind of stress,
Leading me to health
And happiness.

## II. May We be Grateful for Life's Many Gifts

To all my teachers,
I beseech,
Please stay near
and help me teach.

You wisdom helped me
To find my way,
For constant blessings
I will always pray.

To the natural world
That sustains my living
I honor her
For always giving.

Life's bliss and pain
both provide
fertile fields
For wisdom's growth.

## III. May We be Transformed into Our Highest Ideal

This ignorance does
A prison make,
Only true wisdom
Helps me escape.

My many faults
I now confess,
And clear them all
Through forgiveness.

Freedom lies
Inside, not out,
Of this pure truth
I have no doubt.

I know that
Real happiness
Must arise from my
Own consciousness.

Within my being's
Sacred design,
Resides the heart
Of the divine.

## IV. MY WE BE LOVING AND COMPASSIONATE

For those who
Live in misery
I engage in
active empathy.

To help all creatures
To be free,
I place their joy
In front of me.

With love's
Compassionate intent,
I strive for pure
Enlightenment.

The only true
Pain prevention
Is my
Compassionate intention.


## V. May We be Mindful Through Breathing

Mindfully my
Breathing starts,
My consciousness
Goes to my heart.

Within the silence
Of my breath,
There is no birth,
There is no death.

When thoughts
disturb the stillness,
I return
To emptiness.

And then I rest
With tranquil mind
In unity
With the divine.


## VI. May We become Wise Through Meditation

I rest into
A sacred presence
Joined as one

Eternal essence.

The silent wisdom
Keeps me seeing
The loving nature
Of my being.

Sacred light pervades
Me through and through,
And bliss descends
Like mountain dew.

Radiating out,
I now impart
Rainbows of healing
From my heart.

## VII. MAY WE SERVE ALL BEINGS

I send love to friends
And foes who fight
To oppressors and
Oppressed alike.

I see the people
In my life
And vow to help
Overcome their strife.

I vow to sustain
This peace of mind,
To all I meet
I will be kind.

Liberation for all
Is my dedication;
May you be blessed
By this meditation.

# NOTES

1. Kabir Helminski, *The Knowing Heart: A Sufi Path of Transformation*, 98-99; also found in Massud Farzan, *The Tale of the Reed Pipe*, 51-52.

2. In Ecclesiastical Latin, these are pronounced somewhat differently than in Classical Latin. Using a ts sound, they are pronounced, meditatsio, oratsio, and contemplatsio.

3. Thomas Keating, *Foundations for Centering Prayer*, 21. This work contains three works by Keating, including *Open Mind, Open Heart*, from which this quote is taken.

4. The words in brackets here were added for the purpose of clarity.

5. Keating, *Foundations for Centering Prayer*, 22.

6. Psalm 145, as translated by Rabbi Zalman Schachter-Shalomi and Netanel Miles-Yépez in the prayer-book of the Inayati-Maimuni Sufi-Hasidim (private publication).

7. With experience and maturity, meditation leads to an effortless, tranquil focus in which our body, mind, and indeed, our entire being, is at peace. This state does not name itself or announce its presence with words; it is only later when we attempt to explain and interpret this experience to ourselves and others that we use a word or descriptive phrase to identify it. This is where we run into difficulties: once we name and confine a meditation experience to an idea, we easily loose the authenticity of the experience itself and find ourselves arguing about the words rather than returning to the source or cause of the transcendent experience.

8. Heard directly from Father Thomas who was paraphrasing St. John of the Cross. See Thomas Keating, *Intimacy with God*, 55.

9. See Vivekananda, The Yogas and Other Works, 581.

10. Dalai Lama, *Ethics for the New Millennium*, 22.

11. The word "group" is used here because of the rishis of the Hindu tradition, and because all Israel is said to have had the experience at Sinai.

12. Dalai Lama, *Ethics for the New Millennium*, 22.

13. These are words from the Greek, Sanskrit, Hebrew, and Arabic that either mean, 'wisdom' (Gr. *sophia*, San. *prajna*, Heb. *hokhmah*, Ara. *hikmah)*, or 'knowledge' (Gr. *gnosis*, Heb. *da'at*), specifically, 'experiential knowledge.'

14. Rabbi Rami Shapiro, from promotional material for the Spiritual Paths Institute.

15. Thomas Keating, *Manifesting God*, 54-58.

16. Bernie Glassman, *Bearing Witness: A Zen Master's Lessons in Making Peace*, 36.

17. The founding member who was not able to attend was Tania Leontov of Boulder, Colorado, an early student of Chogyam Trungpa Rinpoche.

18. The colors representing the five *samskaras* are blue, white, red, green, and yellow (as seen on Tibetan prayer flags), and represent both the five samskaras (aggregates called form, consciousness, feeling, perception, and formation) and the five elements (space, air, fire, water, earth). Thankas are two-dimensional iconographic depictions of Buddhist exemplars and concepts, often painted

on fabric, and elaborately embroidered. Chenrezig is the Tibetan name for the Bodhisattva usually called Avalokitishvara in Sanskrit.

In Islam, a *mihrab* is a specially designed niche in a structure showing the direction of prayer, i.e., Mecca, in Saudi Arabia. Blue has a special status in Islam, perhaps associated with water for the desert people who were the first Muslims. Calligraphy is an important art form for Muslims, as graphic depictions of the Prophet and Divinity are prohibited. Muslims also use rectangular carpets for prayer, called *sajadas*.

19. For example, the Sufis of Islam may engage in the entrancing movements and chants of the *zikr* to become totally absorbed in the presence of Allah. Yet most Sufi practitioners probably will not claim that their goal is to actually 'become Allah.' On the other hand, a Tibetan Mahayana Buddhist meditator might engage in the Stages of the Path and tantric practices in order to become a Buddha. A mystical Christian might engage in prayer and contemplation to achieve Christ Consciousness by uniting with the Divine Indwelling of the Holy Spirit; but they might not make the claim that they can actually become a Christ. Yet a Hindu meditator might engage in chants and meditation to unite their soul or atman with Brahman or primordial universe creating God. Of course, these are different categories, but the point is that there are different values and approaches in different religions.

20. Western neuropsychological research is beginning to establish scientific criteria to support these ancient claims. F for more resources on this, go to www. mindandlife.org, the website of the Mind and Life Insitute.

21. Also, "the law of reversed effort" and the "backwards law." See Alan W. Watts, *The Wisdom of Insecurity: A Message for an Age of Anxiety.*

22. Johnny Lee, "Lookin' for Love," Urban Cowboy Soundtrack, 1980.

23. See Hirakawa Akira, *A History of Indian Buddhism: From Sakyamuni to Early Mahayana,* 22-23 on the dating of the Buddha's life. Accepting Nakamura Hajime's dating, it is speculated that the Buddha may have lived from 463-383 B.C.E.

24. Translation of His Holiness, Tenzin Gyatso, the 14th Dalai Lama.

25. For more on spiritual eldering, see Zalman Schachter-Shalomi and Ronald S. Miller, *From Age-ing to Sage-ing: A Profound New Vision of Growing Older.*

26. In Jewish mysticism, *Ain Sof,* meaning, 'Without limit,' or 'Infinite Nothing,' is a way of speaking of God; in Buddhism, *Tathagata-garbha,* 'womb of the thus-gone-one,' refers to the innate potential for Buddhahood; and in Hinduism, Brahman, 'the great expansion,' is the Absolute God transcending all concepts.

27. Moses and Buddha are respectively the founding figures of Judaism and Buddhism, while Shankara (also Adi Shankara or Shankaracharya) was the organizer of the doctrine of Advaita Vedanta, the non-dual presentation of the Vedas.

28. Judaism and Islam are the two majors examples of this.

29. Psalm 145, as translated by Rabbi Zalman Schachter-Shalomi and Netanel Miles-Yépez in the prayer-book of the Inayati-Maimuni Sufi-Hasidim (private publication).

30. See Martin Buber, "The Faith of Judaism," *Israel and the World: Essays in a Time of Crisis,* 21-24.

31. Genesis 22:1-24; see Soren Kierkegaard, *Fear and Trembling* for a detailed philosophical unpacking of Abraham's dilemma.

32. Family prayer without reference to a particular god or deity, from an unknown source.

33. Joseph Campbell with Bill Moyers, *The Power of Myth,* 110.

34. Ibid., explained in Schopenhauer's terms.

35. A *bodhisattva* in Mahayana Buddhism is a being who has become 'awakened' and who vows to deliver others from their suffering by helping them to become awakened as well. In China, Avalokitishvara is known as Kuan Yin, in Japan, Kannon, and in Tibet, Chenrezig.

36. Javad Nurbakhsh, *Traditions of the Prophet: Volume 1,* 55, quoting from the *hadith* collection, *Sahih Muslim.*

37. Aside from my Buddhist resources, the most helpful book for me was by Dr. John E. Sarno's *Healing Back Pain, the Mind Body Connection.*

38. Format adapted from Raymond J. DeMallie, ed., *The Sixth Grandfather: Black Elk's Teachings Given to John G. Neihardt,* 126.

39. The first of these two notions is originally based on Leviticus 19:18, "You shall love your neighbor as yourself," but later appears in Mark 12:31, and is also discussed in Luke 10:25-37. The second is found in Matthew 6:39: "[. . .] but whosoever shall smite thee on the right cheek, turn to him the other also."

40. This is a quote from Exodus 21:24 which is often taken out its larger context of equitable consequences for crimes.

41. Through this and other types of thought experimentation, it is possible to deduce the self-serving logic of compassion for others. This logic is now supported by neuro-scientific studies being conducted at several major research centers throughout the world. In these laboratories, both experienced monks and beginning laypersons are instructed to engage in specific meditations on love and compassion. While doing so, their brains are measured by advanced visual imaging and brainwave sensors. The results confirm that the mental intention of love and compassion 'light up' specific parts of the brain proven to correspond with states of calm, tranquility that promote general mental happiness and physical wellness.

42. The 'love your neighbor' intention is based on optimism and hope. The 'eye for an eye' attitude is based on fear. In our times, the absurd and tragic consequence of a fear-based ethic for relationships is exemplified in the strategy of 'mutually assured destruction' between the nations of the world who have nuclear weapons. The continual violence between Israelis and Palestinians and state sponsored terrorism are based on violence and fear. This fear of retribution state of human affairs prevents the development of hope-based policies exemplifying compassionate reciprocity between people who are simply compelled to help each other. I have concluded that the intention of mutually assured generosity must replace the doctrine of mutually assured destruction.

43. The flip-side of this scenario is that a truly good person can also attract the antipathy of a deranged person whose negative self-image compels them to find flaws with a good person or cause them physical harm. The 'eye for an eye' attitude of human consciousness causes some people harm those who exemplify compassion because goodness is a threat to their self image and their personal strategy for survival. History is replete with tragic examples of the assassinations of truly good human beings. Yet, good people persist in the face of danger knowing that the alternative is unacceptable.

44. Based on John 3:16.

45. This is my own concise rendition of the well-known tale from the life of Asanga.

46. Daniel Ladinsky, trans., *The Gift: Poems by Hafiz, the Great Sufi Master,* 333.

47. 1 Corinthians 13: 4-8.

48. This is basically the formula for the Bodhisattva Vow.

49. A quote attributed to Abraham Lincoln in Alexander Kelly McClure, *"Abe" Lincoln's Yarns and Stories,* 184.

50. Inayat Khan, *Gathekas,* "Gatheka 3" (private publication), and Inayat Khan, *The Unity of Religious Ideals,* 68.

51. Format adapted from Muhyiddin ibn al-'Arabi, ed. and trans. Lex Hixon/Nur al-Jerrahi and Fariha Fatima al-Jerrahi, *101 Diamonds from the Oral Tradition of the Glorious Messenger Muhammad,* 141.

52. Some examples are 'spirit' in English, *ruah* in Hebrew, and *ruh* in Arabic.

53. In breathing, we also participate in the marvelous reciprocity of nature, for countless living organisms exhale the oxygen that we must inhale to live, while they likewise inhale the carbon dioxide that we breathe out! Therefore, to meditate on with the breath, contemplating the breath, is to become subtly aware of the intrinsic interdependence and reciprocal nature of all being.

54. See Yogi Nataraja Kallio's article in Part III, "The Breath Within the Breath."

55. The Tibetan word *geshe* is actually a kind of degree earned by scholars of great attainment, and often those who have earned it are called 'Geshe' out of respect, like we might say, 'Dr. so and so,' though it is much more prestigious. *La* is a Tibetan affectionate ending.

56. He also advised me never to use psychotropic drugs because they would disturb and unbalance my subtle energy or *prana,* making it harder to engage in advanced practices later in life.

57. I stayed in the guesthouse belonging to the Dalai Lama's mother. In front of my little room was a lovely yard bordered by three foot high wall to prevent people from straying too close to the very steep hill that descended thousands of feet to the India plains below. I would sit for hours on this wall, looking out on Indian subcontinent that gave birth to Buddhism, making notes in my diary.

58. For a detailed exposition of mindfulness, see Analayo's *Satipatthana, The Direct Path to Realization,* and Joseph Goldstein's *Mindfulness: A Practical Guide to Awakening.*

59. This is not necessarily the physical heart that pumps blood through our body, but according to some traditions, is a place just above and behind our solar plexus that can be located by placing the end of our right little finger in our navel, then stretching our hand upwards over our stomach until the thumb reaches a spot in the solar plexus that is approximately the height of three ribs above the sternum, then two finger widths to the left. There, approximately within the indentation between the third and forth rib from the bottom is the area to which one withdraws one's consciousness. However, this is just one tradition's very particular viewpoint; it may be enough simply to conceive of the heart-center and to place one's awareness in that location. Described to me by Swami Atmarupananda at the Snowmass Interreligious Conference.

60. This is outlined in *The Tibetan Book of the Dead.*

61. Recent brain scans of meditators who are focused on their breathing have even shown positive effects on the neuro-physiology and connectivity within the brain of the meditator.

62. Format adapted from Lao Tsu, trans. Gia-Fu Feng, *Tao Te Ching,* 18. Only the first half of number 16 is given here.

63. See Appendix B: "Way-points on the Contemplative Journey."

64. Although I had been trained in the Buddhist roadmap to spiritual liberation, in my own journey, I have found that the many 'side roads' and 'diversions' available along the way, had not been charted, predicted, or anticipated in any exhaustive way. So one must be personally committed to a meditation practice, anchored in mature reasons for meditating, and open to help and unexpected blessings at all times.

65. See my article "Cultivating Tranquil Focus & Transcendental Insight" in Part III.

66. See Thomas Keating, "The Theological Basis of Centering Prayer," *Intimacy with God,* 32-37.

67. Adapted from Raimundo Panikkar, ed. and trans., *The Vedic Experience – Mantramanjari: An Anthology of the Vedas for Modern Man and Contemporary Celebration,* 676, 679.

68. With support from the National Endowment for the Humanities and a partnership with BBC Television.

69. Sarnath was home to the Buddha's first teachings, now commemorated by an enormous ancient stupa, many temples, and a Tibetan Buddhist institute of higher studies.

70. At the end of every session of meditation or teaching, the Buddhist practitioner 'dedicates the merit' of what has just been accomplished for the benefit of all sentient beings. That is to say, whatever 'benefit' or 'good' was generated by the activity, is not kept for oneself, but is given away to benefit others. However, paradoxically, in giving it away, the practitioner actually accumulates merit!

71. See Miles-Yépez, *The Common Heart,* 37-39, 135.

72. Another version of these ideas are presented in ibid., 38-39.

73. Ibid., 84-85. See also Netanel Miles-Yépez, "Paradigms of Ecumenism as a Spiritual Practice: Father Thomas Keating and Swami Atmarupananda Discuss the Theory and Practice of Dialogue," *Journal of Ecumenical Studies,* 89 where Swami Atmarupananda gives a slightly different account.

74. See section entitled "The Silent Dialogue" in Miles-Yépez, *The Common Heart,* 37-39.

75. Rev. Donald Postema in ibid., 39.

76. This practice can also be done lying down as long as the spine is straight and one can remain alert.

77. Hypertension, neglect, stress, depression, psychological repression all serve to narrow the breath capacity. As we become afflicted by external and psychological challenges, it is a common response to shorten the breath, breathing only through a limited section of the lungs. This results in a host of maladies such as oxygen deprivation, increased carbon dioxide build up and nervous and mental tension. If nothing else, it is essential to learn abdominal breathing (breathing into the

lower lungs which causes the belly to swell on the inhalation and retract on the exhalation) as the majority of oxygen receptors reside in the floor of the lungs, and the parasympathetic nervous system is stimulated.

78. B.K.S. Iyengar, *Light on Pranayama: The Yogic Art of Breathing,* 99.

79. Iyengar, *Light on Pranayama,* 100.

80. Jalal al-Din Rumi, ed. Reynold A. Nicholson, *Masnavi-yi ma'navi,* 36.

81. A later Sufi, Najm al-Din Kubra (d. 1221), explained the remembrance of Allah thus: "The 'h' in the divine name 'Allah' is the very sound we make with every breath. The other letters (in the Arabic spelling: *alif* and reduplicated *lam)* represent an intensified definite article (serving to emphasize the uniqueness of Allah). The essential part of the divine name is therefore that 'h', which automatically accompanies our every breath. All life depends on the constant utterance of that noble name. As for the seeker of intimate knowledge, it is incumbent on him to recognize this subtle fact, and to maintain, with every breath, the consciousness of being with Allah." Mawlana 'Ali ibn Husain Safi, *Rashahat 'Ain al-Hayat: Beads of Dew from the Source of Life,* 18.

82. 'Ali B. Thman Al-Jullabi A Hujwiri, trans. Reynold A. Nicholson, Kashf al-Mahjub of Al Hujwiri: The Oldest Persian Treatise on Sufism, 30-44.

83. Amir Khwurd Kirmani, *Siyar al-awlia',* 448.

84. Shah Kalim Allah Jahanabadi, *Kashkul-i Kalimi,* 31.

85. Inayat Khan, *The Unity of Religious Ideals,* 159.

86. Muhammad Dara Shikuh, ed. and trans. M. Mahfuz-ul-Ha, *Majma'-ul-bahrain.*

87. The *Oxford English Dictionary* defines elementalism as "a method or theory which divinizes the elemental powers of nature."

88. All translations in this chapter are by the author.

89. Late Latin based on the Greek.

90. Greek, 'pouring.' This term is used in Greek philosophy and was later picked up by Christian mystics.

91. As the 'absolute truth', Emptiness connotes an absence of permanence or 'inherent existence.' Things (including the 'soul' or even God) cannot exist on their own because they are interdependent. In fact, even the Buddhist absolute truth "emptiness" is itself empty and interdependent.

92. Late Latin based on the Greek.

# BIBLIOGRAPHY

Analayo. *Satipatthana: The Direct Path to Realization*. Birmingham: Windhorse Publications, 2003.

'Arabi, Muhyiddin ibn al-. *101 Diamonds from the Oral Tradition of the Glorious Messenger Muhammad*. Ed. and Trans. Lex Hixon/Nur al-Jerrahi and Fariha Fatima al-Jerrahi. New York: Pir Press, 2002.

Atisha. *Lamp for the Path to Enlightenment*. Ithaca, NY; Snow Lion, 1997.

Atmarupananda, Swami. *Vedanta: A Religion, A Philosophy, A Way of Life*. Hollywood, California: Vedanta Press, 2010.

Bastian, Edward W., and Tina L. Staley. *Living Fully, Dying Well: Reflecting on Death to Find Your Life's Meaning*. Boulder, Colorado: Sounds True, 2009.

Bourgeault, Cynthia. *Centering Prayer and Inner Awakening*. Boston, MA: Cowley, 2004.

——. *The Wisdom Jesus*. Boston: Shambhala Publications, 2008.

Buber, Martin. *Israel and the World: Essays in a Time of Crisis*. New York: Schocken Books, 1948.

Campbell, Joseph, with Bill Moyers. *The Power of Myth*. Ed. Betty Sue Flowers. New York: Doubleday, 1988.

Dalai Lama. *Essence of the Heart Sutra*. Somerville, Massachusetts: Wisdom Publications, 2005

——. *Ethics for a New Millenium*. New York: Riverhead Books, 1999.

——. *Toward a True Kinship of Faiths: How the World's Religions Can Come Together*. New York, NY: Random House, 2010.

Dalai Lama and Kamalasila. *Stages of Meditation*. Ithaca, NY: Snow Lion, 2003.

DeMallie, Raymond J. ed., *The Sixth Grandfather: Black Elk's Teachings Given to John G. Neihardt*. Lincoln, Nebraska: University of Nebraska Press, 1984.

Farzan, Massud. *The Tale of the Reed Pipe: Teachings of the Sufis*. New York: E.P. Dutton & Co., 1974.

Glassman, Bernie. *Bearing Witness: A Zen Master's Lessons in Making Peace*. New York: Bell Tower, 1998.

Goldstein, Joseph. *Mindfulness: A Practical Guide to Awakening*. Boulder, CO: Sounds True, 2013.

Helminski, Kabir. *The Knowing Heart: A Sufi Path of Transformation*. Boston: Shambhala Publications, 1999.

Hirakawa Akira. *A History of Indian Buddhism: From Sakyamuni to*

*Early Mahayana*. Ed. and Trans. Paul Groner. Delhi: Motilal Banarsidass Publishers, 1998.

Hujwiri, 'Ali B. Thman al-Jullabi al-. *Kashf al-Mahjub of Al Hujwiri: The Oldest Persian Treatise on Sufism*. Trans. Reynold A. Nicholson. London: Luzac and Co., 1976.

Iyengar, B.K.S.. *Light on Pranayama: The Yogic Art of Breathing*. New York: Crossroad Publishing Company, 1989.

Jahanabadi, Shah Kalim Allah. *Kashkul-i Kalimi*. Delhi: Matba'-i Mujtaba'i, n.d..

Keating, Thomas. *Foundations for Centering Prayer and the Christian Contemplative Life: Open Mind, Open Heart; Invitation to Love; The Mystery of Christ*. New York: Continuum, 2002.

——. *Intimacy with God*. New York: Crossroad Publishing Co., 1994.

——. *Manifesting God*. New York: Lantern Books, 2005.

Khan, Inayat. *Sufi Teachings*. Delhi: Motilal Banarsidass Publishers, 2003.

——. *The Unity of Religious Ideals*. London: The Sufi Movement, 1921.

Kierkegaard, Soren. *Fear and Trembling*. Trans. Alastair Hannay. Penguin Books, New York: 1985.

Kirmani, Amir Khwurd. *Siyar al-awlia'*. Delhi: Matba'-i Muhibb-i Hind, 1885.

Ladinsky, Daniel, trans., *The Gift: Poems by Hafiz, the Great Sufi Master*. New York: Penguin Compass, 1999.

Laird, Martin. *Into the Silent Land*. Oxford, England: Oxford University Press, 2006.

Lao Tsu. *Tao Te Ching*. Trans. Gia-Fu Feng and Jane English. New York: Vintage Books, 1989.

McClure, Alexander Kelly. *"Abe" Lincoln's Yarns and Stories*. New York: Western W. Wilson, 1901.

Miles-Yépez, Netanel, ed.. *The Common Heart: An Experience of Interreligious Dialogue*. New York: Lantern Books, 2006.

——. "Paradigms of Ecumenism as a Spiritual Practice: Father Thomas Keating and Swami Atmarupananda Discuss the Theory and Practice of Dialogue." *Journal of Ecumenical Studies*. Vol. 43, No. 1; Winter, 2008.

Nurbakhsh, Javad. *Traditions of the Prophet: Volume 1*. New York: Khaniqahi-Nimatullahi Publications, 1981.

Panikkar, Raimundo et al, ed. and trans.. *The Vedic Experience – Mantramanjari: An Anthology of the Vedas for Modern Man and Contemporary Celebration*. Berkeley: University of California Press, 1977.

Progoff, Ira, ed. *The Cloud of Unknowing.* New York: Delta Books, 1957.

Rahula, Wapola. *What the Buddha Taught.* New York, NY: Random House, 1962.

Rumi, Jalal al-Din. *Masnavi-yi ma'navi.* Ed. Reynold A. Nicholson. Tehran: Intisharat-i Bihnud, 1953/4.

Safi, Mawlana 'Ali ibn Husain. *Rashahat 'Ain al-Hayat: Beads of Dew from the Source of Life.* Trans. Muhtar Holland. Ft. Lauderdale, Florida: Al-Baz Publications, 2001.

Sarno, John E.. *Healing Back Pain: The Mind Body Connection.* New York: Warner Books, 1991.

Schachter-Shalomi, Zalman, and Ronald S. Miller. *From Age-ing to Sage-ing: A Profound New Vision of Growing Older.* New York: Warner Books, 1995.

Shantideva. *The Way of the Bodhisattva.* Trans. Padmakara Translation Group. Boston: Shambhala Publications, 1997.

Shapiro, Rami. *The Way of Solomon: Finding Joy and Contentment in the Wisdom of Ecclesiastes.* San Francisco, California: HarperCollins, 2000.

Shikuh, Muhammad Dara. *Majma'-ul-bahrain.* Ed. and Trans. M. Mahfuz-ul-Haq. Calcutta: The Asiatic Society, 1982.

Sopa, Geshe Lhundup. *Steps on the Path to Enlightenment.* Somerville, MA: Wisdom, 2004.

Teasdale, Wayne. *The Mystic Heart: Discovering a Universal Spirituality in the World's Religions.* Novato, California: New World Library, 1999.

Thich Nhat Hanh. *Peace is in Every Step: The Path of Mindfulness in Everyday Life.* New York: Bantam, 1991.

Vivekananda. *The Yogas and Other Works: Revised Edition.* Ed. Nikhilananda. New York: Ramakrishna-Vivekananda Center, 1953.

Vrajaprana, Pravrajika. *Vedanta: A Simple Introduction.* Hollywood, California: Vedanta Press, 1999.

Watts, Alan W.. *The Wisdom of Insecurity: A Message for an Age of Anxiety.* Pantheon, 1951.

# Acknowledgments

THERE ARE SO MANY FRIENDS, supporters and colleagues who have been a part of this endeavor that I wish to thank. I will simply mention their names here without being specific as to why. Sadly, I will have forgotten some significant names that later editions will include. Please forgive me if yours is one of these. My deep gratitude to Reverend Gregg Anderson, Swami Atmarupananda, Alexandra Bastian, Jonathan Bastian, Marianne Bastian, Reverend Lauren Atress, John Bennett, Rabbi Ozer Bergman, Rev. Diane Berke, Tessa Bielecki, Harvey Bottelsen, Bikkhu Bodhi, Joan Borysenko, Reverend Cynthia Bourgeault, Mary Ann Brussat, Loya Cespooch, Nancy Belle Coe, Sister Brahmaprana, Ken Cohen, Katherine and Roger Collis, Kathy Corcoran, Anita Daniel, Father Dave Denny, Kelly Dignan, Laura Dixon, Geshe Lobsang Donyo, Gordon Dveirin, Suzanne Farver, Mollie Favour, Rob Gabriel, Gelek Rinpoche, Stephanie Glatt, Dr. John Allen Grimes, Richard Groves, Roshi Joan Halifax, Sheikh Kabir and Camille Helminski, Rabbi Brad Hirschfield, Sister Jose Hobday, James Hughes, Judy Hyde, Pir Zia Inayat-Khan, Edie Irons, Don "Four Arrows" Jacobs, Reverend Alan Jones, Chief Oren Lyons, Yogi Nataraja Kallio, Father Thomas Keating, Rabbi Miles Krassen, Dr. Michael Kearney, Paul Keeley, Reverend Master Khoten, Acharya Judy Lief, Rev. Aaron McEmrys, Dena Merriam, Brad Miller, Sheikh Muhammad Jamal al-Jerrahi (Gregory Blann), Rabbi Leah Novick, Lexie Potamkin, Reverend Tenzin Priyadarshi, Margot and Tom Pritzker, Lynda Rae, Imam Feisal Abdul Rauf, Jonathan and Diana Rose, Rabbi Jeff Roth, Sharon Salzburg, Barbara Sargent, Swami Sarvadevananda, Rabbi Zalman Schachter-Shalomi, Rabbi Arthur Gross Schaefer, Dr. Marilyn Schlitz, Christianne Schlumberger, Grace Alvarez Sesma, Rabbi Rami Shapiro, Acharya Judith Simmer-Brown, Ajahn Sona, Geshe Lhundup Sopa, Tina Staley, Michael Stranahan, Tekaronianeken Jake Swamp, Brother Wayne Teasdale, Geshe Lobsang Tenzin, Juliet Spohn-Twomey, Ani Tenzin Kacho, Lauren Van Ham, Pravrajika Vrajaprana, Dr. B. Alan Wallace, Radhule Weininger, Sharon Wells, Catherine Wyler, and Paula Zurcher.

I am also grateful to all those who have studied InterSpiritual Meditation with me, for they have helped to clarify and refine the ideas and practices described herein. I also wish to thank Amitai Zachary Malone, for proofing the text, and Netanel Miles-Yépez, the editor of this book, who has been an invaluable friend and colleague on the journey of Spiritual Paths.

# THE SPIRITUAL PATHS INSTITUTE

SPIRITUAL PATHS convenes a distinguished faculty to educate and train students in the principles, theories and practices of meditation and contemplation from the world's great spiritual traditions. We call this work "InterSpiritual" because of the unique process of group meditations and our continuing dialogue around contemplative intentions, methods, and experiences. Working together, we co-create an inner foundation for active engagement in the world. Our programs and educational materials help participants develop a sustainable contemplative practice, benefit from the wisdom of various traditions, and create a community of people from many spiritual perspectives to solve the challenges of our time.

The exceptional value of the Spiritual Paths Institute comes from an integrated training in a primary practice along with systematic exposure to practices from other traditions. This uniquely inclusive education and training helps students to develop a mature, comprehensive, and sustainable meditative practice, giving rise to compassion, wisdom, equanimity, meaning, and purpose. Each of our educational and public service projects are based on these principles. The goal of all our programs is to develop universal InterSpiritual Wisdom to guide us in our personal lives, relationships, professions, and service in the world.

## COURSES IN INTERSPIRITUAL MEDITATION

InterSpiritual Meditation is a process where people of all spiritual perspectives and traditions, including agnostics and atheists, can discover common ground for solving the challenges of our times. We are finding that shared contemplative experience can provide a foundation for peace, respect, health, justice, and the flourishing of our full human potential. Our courses and online forums explore the context, principles, theories, and methods underlying the practice of meditation within the world's major spiritual traditions. Our goal is to help you develop the foundation for a mature and sustainable meditation practice. To learn more about our InterSpiritual Meditation courses and seminars, visit: www.interspiritualmeditation.org, or e-mail Edward Bastian at ed@spiritualpaths.net.

# ABOUT THE AUTHOR

DR. EDWARD W. BASTIAN holds a Ph.D. in Buddhist Studies and is the founder and president of the Spiritual Paths Foundation. His current writing and teaching is the product of over forty years of research and study, especially in the last decades with over fifty esteemed teachers of Buddhism, Christianity, Hinduism, Islam, Judaism, Taoism, and Native American traditions. He is the award winning co-author of *Living Fully Dying Well* (2009), author of *InterSpiritual Meditation* (2010), and producer of various documentaries on religion for the BBC and PBS.

Bastian is the former co-director of the Forum on BioDiversity for the Smithsonian and National Academy of Sciences, teacher of Buddhism and world religions at the Smithsonian, an Internet entrepreneur and translator of Buddhist scriptures from Tibetan into English. He is also an Adjunct Professor at Antioch University in Santa Barbara where he is teaching courses on Buddhism and Mindfulness Meditation, and Fielding Graduate University where he teaches Contemplative Leadership. Bastian also teaches on-line courses as well as seminars and retreats at such organizations as One Spirit Interfaith, Chaplaincy Institute, CIIS, Sacred Art of Living and Dying, Interspiritual Centre of Vancouver, Cascadia Center, Esalen Institute, Omega Institute, Hollyhock Retreat Center, Garrison Institute and La Casa de Maria.

He is the Co-President of the Interfaith Initiative of Santa Barbara, co-founder of ECOFaith Santa Barbara and Trustee of the United Religions Initiative Global Council.

Made in United States
Troutdale, OR
06/18/2024

20649089R00139